SEVENTEEN
TO MILLIONAIRE

2024

Library and Archives Canada Cataloguing in Publication Price, Douglas, 1987 — Seventeen To Millionaire: You're seventeen, You're Canadian, You wanna be rich, Let's do this.

Issued also in electronic and audio formats.

ISBN 978-1-7780592-0-9

Finance, Personal, I, Title.

SEVENTEEN
TO MILLIONAIRE

DOUGLAS PRICE

CHUNKS

CHUNK 1: The Golden Rules 1

    LET'S BE CRYSTAL CLEAR 3

    I KNEW (PRETTY MUCH) NOTHING 5

    THE AVERAGE CANADIAN. 7

    WHERE DO YOU START? 9

    HOW DO YOU INVEST MONEY? 11

    BANKS 14

    BROKERAGES 18

    INVESTING ACCOUNTS. 22

    BEFORE WE CONTINUE 24

    GOLDEN RULE #1: THE 10% RULE 26

    THREE AGREEMENTS 30

    GOLDEN RULE #2: MAX OUT YOUR TFSA. 33

    LEVEL-UP ON TFSAs 38

    GOLDEN RULE #3: SNOWBALL COMPOUND INTEREST . . 47

    YOUR PARENTS #1 53

    THE GOLDEN RECAP 55

CHUNK 2: The Ski Slope. 57

    FASTER OR SLOWER. 59

    IN A NUTSHELL: THE STOCK MARKET 62

    IN A NUTSHELL: BONDS. 65

    IN A NUTSHELL: FUNDS 70

    IN A NUTSHELL: MUTUAL FUNDS 73

    IN A NUTSHELL: INDEX FUNDS 78

    IN A NUTSHELL: EXCHANGE-TRADED FUNDS 81

    IN A NUTSHELL: STOCKS 84

    A NOTE ABOUT INVESTING IN STOCKS 91

    DOUG'S DEFAULT INVESTMENT PLAN 93

    DOLLAR-COST AVERAGING 95

IN A NUTSHELL: DIVIDENDS. 100
LEVEL-UP ON DIVIDENDS. 104
YOUR PARENTS #2 106

CHUNK 3: The Road Trip 109
PIT STOP #1: YOU'RE HIRED. 111
TAXED AT THE SOURCE 114
YOUR PAY STUB 117
PIT STOP #2: TAX BRACKETS. 125
DON'T MAKE THIS MISTAKE! 132
PIT STOP #3: TOTAL INCOME & TAXABLE INCOME 136
REGISTERED RETIREMENT SAVINGS PLAN 140
LEVEL-UP ON RRSPs #1 149
LEVEL-UP ON RRSPs #2 153
LEVEL-UP ON RRSPs #3 156
LEVEL-UP ON RRSPs #4 (TAX REFUNDS) 162
GAME NIGHT 166

CHUNK 4: The World of Credit. 169
THE WORLD OF CREDIT 171
CREDIT CARDS 175
LEVEL-UP ON CREDIT CARDS 182
LINES OF CREDIT 187
LEVEL-UP ON LINES OF CREDIT 194
YOUR PARENTS #3 201

CHUNK 5: Tax Slips & Life Tips 203
IN A NUTSHELL: TAX SLIPS. 205
THE T4 TAX SLIP 208
THE T2202 TAX SLIP 214
TAX CREDITS 222
FOR QUÉBEC'S EYES ONLY THE RELEVÉ TAX SLIPS 230
STUDENT DEBT 237

KEEPING A BUDGET 241

YOUR CRA MY ACCOUNT. 246

INSURANCE 249

WHO NEEDS INSURANCE?. 251

GIVING MONEY AWAY 254

SO... WHY? 257

BOWING OUT. 260

THE TO-DO LIST (6 items) 262

IMPORTANT DATES. 265

RIDICULOUS TERMS 266

THE MATH 271

SHOUT OUT TO COOL PEOPLE 273

WHO EXACTLY IS THIS DOUG GUY? 276

This book is dedicated to a Future Millionaire.

Hey, wait. That's you!

Sweet.

CHUNK 1
THE GOLDEN RULES

LET'S BE CRYSTAL CLEAR

Money? Finances? Saving?

Boring.

I know what you're thinking:

"Interesting book title…but is this gonna be another book by some old dude who drones on about dry, mind-numbing topics in a monotonous, slightly nasal voice?"

Trust me, I get it. This is not that book. Although, easy for me to say—I wrote it.

So let's make a deal:

You read to page 55. (Approx. reading time: 29 minutes.)

If by that point you're unimpressed and uninterested, then hey, no worries. This isn't for you.

In fact, let me be crystal clear:

This book was written for the seventeen-year-old Canadian who prides themselves in having a shred of common sense, who's not afraid to work hard, and who aspires to create wealth, retire early, and reach millionaire status.

If that's not you, then cool. Walk away.

See ya.

But if that is you…

…then let's do this.

I KNEW (PRETTY MUCH) NOTHING

I don't have a finance background.

I don't have a finance degree. I've never worked for a bank or finance company. I've never "officially" financially advised anyone.

Hell, I've never even walked the entire length of Wall Street in New York.

If you're expecting credentials, certificates, degrees, and other shiny bits of paper meant to show off my level of financial competency…

You got the wrong guy. That ain't me.

Here's what happened:

In 2017, I threw up my hands in frustration at my lack of knowledge about money.

Where do people learn this stuff?! Why is it *so* complicated?!

And why the HELL was I not taught this in high school?!?!

Angry table flip

The journey began.

I bought books, watched DVDs, and enrolled in courses.

I watched YouTube videos and asked about a million questions to people much more knowledgeable than me.

Slowly, I pieced it together.

After four years of hard work, I started writing.

This is my accumulation of knowledge after thousands of hours of studying Canada's financial systems, managing and growing my own investments, and designing and teaching a finance course for the school I used to work at.

Here's the disclaimer, the heads-up:

DO NOT CONSIDER THIS
OFFICIAL FINANCIAL ADVICE.

Take everything I say with a grain of salt. And please, please do your own research.

With that said, I hope you find this book useful. If only to justify the twenty-three bucks.

If it ain't useful, well hey, at least it wasn't twenty-four.

You should also know: I had a kick-ass time writing this book.

I hope you have a kick-ass time reading it.

THE AVERAGE CANADIAN

You're seventeen. You're in high school. Let me ask you:

How much have you learned about investing money, growing wealth, and becoming a millionaire?

> Exactly.

Your parents, by your age, probably learned about the same amount.

Canadians, in my experience, are embarrassingly undereducated when it comes to understanding money. And it's not entirely their fault. We're not taught!

As a result, millions of Canadians would love to be rich…

> *But they don't know how.*

Or they're not prepared to really work for it.

Except here's the thing: You can become a millionaire flipping burgers at your local fast-food joint.

Sure, it'd take some time and some work, but it's possible. Like, 100% possible.

I'm gonna show you how. And you know what?

You can do it.

Yes, my friend. *You can do it.*

Canadians have many tools available to help them grow their money.

But here's the problem:

If you don't know the tools exist or how they function, how are you expected to make them work for you?!

That's like wanting to put a nail into a wall without knowing that hammers exist. Good luck.

This book is designed to show you the hammers.

WHERE DO YOU START?

Right here. Let's go.

When you make money, you have four options. You can:

1) SPEND it on stuff.

2) PAY OFF debts.

3) GIVE it away.

4) SAVE/INVEST it.

Spending is the fun one. Obviously. Let's buy stuff on Amazon! Woot woot!

Paying off debts is less fun. But super important.

Giving it away…this one might surprise you. But we'll come back to it.

Saving/Investing. Most of the book focuses on this one.

Can I be honest? I hate the word "saving."

It sounds like something my grandmother would say. "Save it for a rainy day." ***eye roll***

Also, when I hear the word "save," as in "to save money," I have this image in my mind of someone stuffing $10 bills into a sock drawer.

If that's you, don't worry. You're seventeen. It's okay.

(In fact, if you're seventeen and stuffing $10 bills into a sock drawer, that's brilliant.)

But when you turn eighteen, no more sock drawer, okay?

Things get real.

So because I hate the word "saving," from now on we're gonna use the word "investing." It sounds cooler.

Because if you're "investing money," you're "becoming rich."

And if you're "becoming rich" at your age, then holy hell, you're a badass.

Let me spill the beans:

Investing money is the only way to become a millionaire.

HOW DO YOU INVEST MONEY?

Think of a company you like. I'll give you a second.

Do you have one in mind? Okay, pretend you phone them up and say this:

> *"Hey, Company I like, I think you're awesome. Take my money and use it to become bigger and awesomer!"*

The company responds:

> *"You want us to take your money and use it to become bigger and awesomer?? Yes. We can do that!"*

Then you say:

> *"But you're just borrowing my money. And when I want it back, I'm gonna expect you to give me back more money than I first gave you."*

That's investing. More or less.

You lend a company or organization your money. They grow and expand.

When you want your money back, ideally, they give you back more money than you gave them.

So how do you do this?

I know what you're thinking and no, you can't just walk into your favourite store and start handing them cash.

I like Tesla, but I'm not about to walk into a dealership and start chucking hundred-dollar bills at the salespeople.

(Although can you imagine their faces? So confused. "What…are you doing?!")

In order to invest in a company or organization, you need to open a special kind of account called an "investing account," also known as a "brokerage account."

This is different from what you might already have at your bank.

Do you already have a "checking account" or "savings account"?

If you're thinking, "Uh…I just have a regular bank account," then it's probably one of those.

An "investing account" is different.

In order to open one of these fancy investing accounts you need a brokerage.

Good news: most banks have a brokerage department.

> Future Millionaire: "Whoa, hold up, Doug, slow down. Brokerage department? What the heck is a brokerage?!"

Here's the thing: There are banks and there are brokerages.

They're different. But they're often under the same roof.

Try to separate them in your mind. Two different things, often one building.

BANKS ‖ BROKERAGES

Let's pause our investing chat for a second. We'll come back to it.

First, let's understand what we're dealing with here.

BANKS

I awkwardly said this to a banker once:

> "Aren't banks just really tall buildings with people in suits doing fancy money things?"

She was like, "Uh...sorta."

But how do these really tall buildings with fancy money people make billions of dollars?

In a nutshell, here's how it works:

You have the Bank and then you have two groups of people: Group A and Group B.

The Bank says to the people in Group A, "Hey Group A, why don't you all open bank accounts with me, put your money inside those accounts, and I'll protect it and keep it safe."

Group A is like, "Keep our money safe? That sounds good! Okay, let's do it!"

So Group A goes to the Bank, opens a bunch of bank accounts, and puts their money inside them.

So far so good?

Then Group B comes along and is like, "I really need money to pay for university or to buy a house or a boat or something really expensive."

The Bank looks at Group B and says, "Hey Group B, I have all this money sitting here from Group A…I guess…if you wanted…you could, like, borrow it? But it's Group A's money…so you'd have to pay it back. All of it. Plus, a little bit extra."

Group B is like, "Yeah, that sounds good!"

So the Bank lends the money to Group B, who has to eventually pay it back, dollar for dollar, plus a little bit extra.

We call this little bit extra the "interest."

(It should really be called "The little-bit-extra-you-have-to-pay-for-the-convenience-of-borrowing-the-money-in-the-first-place"…clearly they didn't ask me.)

So Group B pays the money back to the bank, plus the little bit extra, the interest.

And when this happens, the Bank keeps the interest.

Let's break it down with some numbers.

Say the people in Group A put a total of $100 into their accounts.

Group B needs to borrow $100.

The Bank says to Group B, "You can borrow the $100 at 10% interest."

This means Group B has to pay back the $100 plus 10%, which would be $10.

Pretty simple, right?

But hang on. Where did that $100 come from in the first place?

Group A. You got it.

It wasn't the Bank's money. It was Group A's money!

All those nice people in Group A think they've put their money into a bank account, and it's supposed to be sitting in a vault somewhere at the bank.

Wrong.

The Bank is lending it out to people in Group B!

So Group B "borrows $100 at 10% interest." They pay back $110.

Now Group A decides they want to take out their original $100.

What's the Bank left with?

$10.

The Bank just made $10 off Group A's $100!

But what if Group A doesn't take out their money?

Well, then the Bank can keep lending the same $100 to Group B again and again and again. Every time making $10.

This, in a nutshell, is how banks make billions.

But wait! Weren't you told as a kid that the bank will pay you to keep your money there?

…yeah…

In our example, the bank keeps the 10% interest.

Technically, yes, it's true, the bank passes on a tiny, tiny, tiny bit of the interest to you as a little "hey, thanks for letting us lend out your money and make billions off it."

The amount they pass on to you is so tiny, most people don't notice it. I certainly don't.

So don't be fooled into thinking you're gonna get rich by simply keeping your money in a regular bank account.

You won't. Full stop.

That's like holding the nail up to the wall and waiting for it to hammer itself in.

Regular bank account = Not gettin' rich.

Instead, you need an investing account.

With a brokerage.

BROKERAGES

A brokerage is the middleman for buyers and sellers.

I'll explain.

Think of another company you like. Are you a pop drinker?
Do you like Coca-Cola? Just for a sec, let's assume you do.

Coca-Cola is a huge company. Like, enormous.

Think of the Coca-Cola company as a massive pie divided
into millions and millions of tiny slices. If you wanted, you
could buy one of those tiny slices.

We call it a stock.

I know you've heard of "stocks and bonds," blah blah blah.
I'll get into that later. What matters now is this:

Right now, this very second, there's someone in the world
who wants to buy a slice of Coca-Cola.

Conveniently, right now, this very second, there's also someone who wants to sell their slice of Coca-Cola.

A brokerage helps both parties get what they want.

You go through a brokerage to sell your slice of a company.

You go through a brokerage to buy your slice of a company.

Why am I telling you this?

When you're "investing money," you're buying.

I'll say that again.

When you're "investing money," you're buying.

When you put money into an investing account (with a brokerage), you're going to *buy* something with that money.

Maybe a slice of Coca-Cola.

And we hope that, over time, whatever you buy increases in value.

Like, if you buy a slice of Coca-Cola, we hope that the entire Coca-Cola pie gets bigger.

If the pie does indeed get bigger, then your slice gets bigger.

It's still the same percentage of the overall pie, it's just the pie has grown. Bigger pie, bigger slices.

So when you're investing, you're buying slices.

And there are tons of things you can buy (or "invest in"). Yes, certainly stocks and bonds, blah blah blah, but lots of other things too.

Again, much more on that later.

The point is this:

In order to be rich, you need to invest money.

In order to invest money, you need an investing account.

In order to have an investing account, you need a brokerage.

Now, like I said, banks and brokerages are often under the same roof. It is highly likely your bank has a brokerage department.

If your bank does not have its own brokerage, it's time to start looking for one. There are all kinds of platforms online that offer brokerage services. Start googling.

But let's assume your bank does have a brokerage department (since most of them do).

Here are four simple steps to begin the process of opening an investing account:

1) Walk into your bank.

2) Say to the bank teller, "Hi, I'd like to open up an investing account to start investing."

3) The teller will say, "Sure, I can set up a meeting with one of our financial advisors." (Someone once asked me if you had to pay for a meeting. Nope! It's free!)

4) At your meeting, the financial advisor will ask you, "What kind of investing account would you like to open?"

That's when you think, "There are different kinds?! Oh crap, I should've read further in that *Seventeen To Millionaire* book... um..."

Don't worry. I got your back. Keep reading.

You're doing great.

PS. I asked one of our test readers if, after reading this chapter, she'd be able to explain the concept of a brokerage to someone else.

She said, "Sure, a brokerage takes the slice of pie from the plate of the seller and puts it onto the plate of the buyer."

Yup. Brilliant. That's pretty much it.

INVESTING ACCOUNTS

So what do you say to the banker when they ask:

"What kind of investing account would you like to open?"

You have two categories of options:

REGISTERED || NON-REGISTERED

"Registered" basically means the government helps keep track of your account.

"Non-registered" means the government does not keep track of it, and the rules regarding taxes are slightly different.

For now, we're only going to focus on the "Registered" types of accounts and ignore the "Non-Registered."

Trust me on this.

There's a whole bunch of Registered accounts. Here are some you may have heard of:

- Tax-Free Savings Account (TFSA)
- Registered Retirement Savings Plan (RRSP)
- Registered Education Savings Plan (RESP)
- Registered Retirement Income Fund (RRIF)

The ONLY one I want you to focus on is the first one; the Tax-Free Savings Account (TFSA). Ignore the rest. For now.

I'll do a quick formal introduction:

Future Millionaire, meet Tax-Free Savings Account.

Tax-Free Savings Account, meet Future Millionaire.

The two of you are going to be the best of friends.

BEFORE WE CONTINUE

Do you have a job?

Yes? Sweet.

No? That's okay! At least, for the purposes of this book, that's okay.

Here's the thing:

This book was not written to help you find a job. There are already tons of books out there for that.

This book assumes you already have a bit of money coming your way. Whether it's from a job or an allowance, doesn't matter.

Again, if you have absolutely zip coming at you right now (no job, no allowance), don't panic.

Just for fun, let's assume you have a job and you're making a bit of money.

How can you use some of that money to guarantee you'll become a millionaire?

(Notice I said "some." You only need a small portion of it, regularly, to hit millionaire status.)

There are THREE GOLDEN RULES. Only three!

And on the following pages, I will reveal them to you.

You're welcome.

Also, here is my promise:

> *I, Douglas Price, promise you _____*
> *(seventeen-year-old reader), if you rigorously—and*
> *I mean rigorously—follow these THREE GOLDEN*
> *RULES, barring some total catastrophe, at some*
> *point in your life, you will be a millionaire.*

That is my promise.

I'll tell you what to do. You do it. At some point, you become a millionaire.

Sound good?

You ready?

Buckle up.

GOLDEN RULE #1

THE 10% RULE

This is also known as the "Pay Yourself First" rule.

Once I explain this, it's gonna sound super obvious. And yet millions of Canadians don't do it.

"Why not?" you ask. I…don't…know…

The basic idea is this: Save 10% of all the money you make.

(Sorry, yes, you're right, I promised we weren't going to use the word "save." My bad.)

Let's try this again: *Invest* 10% of all the money you make. That's better.

Let's say you make $100 working at McDonald's.

Take 10% ($10) and put it in an investing account. (Like a Tax-Free Savings Account. More on that in Golden Rule #2.)

That's all you gotta do! That's it! Take 10% of the money you make and invest it. It's almost too easy!

But people have it backwards. Most people do this:

1) They make $100. 2) They spend $100. 3) They have nothing left to invest.

We gotta switch up the order!

1) They make $100. 2) They invest $10. 3) They spend the rest.

This is a small mental adjustment, but it makes a *massive* difference.

Earn Money >>> Invest 10% >>> Spend the rest

And I know what you're thinking: "But Doug, that means I'll have $10 less to spend!"

Guess what? You won't even notice. Trust me. Studies have been done.

And here's the best part: You can get your bank to do this automatically for you, so you never have to think about it.

It's called an "automatic deposit."

Here's how it works:

Every time you get a paycheque deposited into your bank account, the bank automatically takes a certain amount (10%) and transfers it to your investing account.

Which means you literally never have to think about it.

Set it and forget it. Love it.

Ask your banker about this. They'll know exactly what you're talking about.

Say something like:

"I'd like to set up an automatic deposit which takes 10% of my paycheque—whatever that specific dollar amount is—and deposits the money into my Tax-Free Savings Account."

(It's coming up, don't worry.)

If you do this, if you set up automatic deposits with 10% of your paycheque, you're brilliant.

This basically *guarantees* you a winning lottery ticket in about twenty years. You'll thank me.

I'm gonna really drive this point home:

> *Investing 10% of your money is essential*
> *to becoming a millionaire.*

And like I said, you won't even notice that 10% difference in your spending money. I promise.

Fine, *maybe one or two times* you don't buy the popcorn and snacks at the movies with your friends.

> If they're smart, they'll understand.

If they give you a hard time, well, let's compare situations in twenty years when you're sitting on a mountain of cash.

And you can tell them, "I read this awesome book to help me become a millionaire by this brilliant guy named Doug Price."

(It doesn't have to be word-for-word.)

So that's GOLDEN RULE #1: THE 10% RULE.

Invest 10% of the money you make.

You're gonna take that money and put it into an investing account.

Remember the Tax-Free Savings Account I introduced you to? It's coming up in Golden Rule #2.

But first, before we get there, let's agree on a few things…

THREE AGREEMENTS

Before we get to Golden Rule #2, there are three things we need to agree on.

AGREEMENT #1:

Every time you earn money, you don't get to keep all of it. You gotta pay a portion of it in taxes to the government. It's the law. Sorry.

How much of it do you have to pay?

That depends. More on that later. For now, let's keep it simple:

Let's say, when you make money, you have to pay 20% of it in taxes.

That means every time you make $100, you have to give $20 to the government, and you get to keep the other $80.

I know, it sucks. But that's the price we pay for the privilege of living in Canada. It's a trade-off.

That's Agreement #1. Whenever you make money, you gotta pay taxes. So far so good?

AGREEMENT #2:

Ideally, when you invest money, it will make you more money.

Does that make sense?

You invest money. The money you invest will (hopefully) grow and grow and earn you more money. Money making money.

This is awesome. And it's how the rich get richer. Their invested money is making them more money!

That's sweet.

In fact, get this: With enough money invested, you can get to a point where *your invested money is making you more money than your day job is!*

I'd say that's a pretty nice problem to have.

So that's Agreement #2: Your invested money makes you more money. (Ideally.)

AGREEMENT #3 (the tricky one, pay close attention!):

When your invested money makes you more money, you have to pay tax on the new money you made.

Read that again. Wrap your mind around it. It's tricky, but very important to understand.

Let's say you invest $100. And after a year, it's up to $110. So your invested money made you $10.

If you're taxed at 20% (like in AGREEMENT #1), then that means you must, by law, give $2 to the government.

Make sense?

Your invested money made you $10. You gotta pay tax on it. You gotta pay 20%. You gotta pay $2.

In other words:

You invest money. Your invested money makes you more money. You don't get to keep all of the new money; you gotta pay some of it in tax.

That's Agreement #3.

If you understand those three agreements (and...you agree), then rock on!

It's time to talk about Golden Rule #2.

GOLDEN RULE #2

MAX OUT YOUR TFSA

Are those THREE AGREEMENTS from the last chapter still fresh in your mind? Do they make sense?

If yes, then let's go.

TFSA stands for "Tax-Free Savings Account."

You remember how I hate the word "saving" and prefer the word "investing"?

It's the same here.

The "Tax-Free Savings Account" should really be called the "Tax-Free *Investing* Account" because when you put money into this account, you're *investing*.

Here's how it works:

You open a TFSA at your bank/brokerage and put money into it. For now, we'll say this money is "invested."

Your invested money inside your TFSA makes you more money, just like in AGREEMENT #2.

But remember AGREEMENT #3? Normally, you would be taxed on all that new money your invested money is making you…

But not with a Tax-Free Savings Account.

When you invest using a TFSA, all the money you make inside the account is tax-free! You don't have to pay tax on it!

Trust me, this is awesome. Check it out using our previous example:

You invest $100 into your TFSA. After a year, it's up to $110.

So you made $10.

Normally, as we discussed, you would have to pay $2 in taxes to the government. But now…you don't.

Now it's all tax-free because you used
a Tax-Free Savings Account!

You get to keep the *entire $10.* Boom! How epic is that?!

Okay, okay, okay, I know what you're thinking: "Doug, it's $10, who cares?"

Sure.

But let's change our example to show you just how awesome TFSAs are.

Let's say you invest $50,000 using your TFSA. And let's say you leave it in the account for ten years.

We know money makes money.

So your $50,000 would make you more money, which would make you more money, which would make you more money, which would make—you get the point.

And let's say after ten years, your $50,000 has turned into $120,000 (completely possible).

That means you started with $50,000, you did *nothing* for ten years, and now you have $120,000.

You made $70,000 out of thin air!

So normally, you'd have to hand over a huge chunk of that money to the government.

But now…you don't.

Instead, when you withdraw (take out) the money, all $120,000 of that money is tax-free! You get to keep all of it!

That's because you used a TFSA.

So you don't have to send ANY of it to the government!

This is amazing.

AND… it's completely legal! Booyah!

So this is great. But how do we actually do this?

Here's the thing: You can only open a TFSA when you turn eighteen years old.

(In some provinces/territories you have to be nineteen. I'll tell you which ones on the next page.)

This is one of the main reasons why this book was written for the seventeen-year-old Canadian; to prepare you to begin investing as early in your life as possible.

Here's what you gotta do:

1) On your eighteenth birthday, before the cake and ice cream, walk into your bank.

2) Tell them it's your birthday (hopefully they won't sing) and ask to "schedule a meeting with a financial advisor for the purpose of opening a Tax-Free Savings Account."

If you do this—*if you actually do this*—it will be one of the greatest decisions you make in your entire life.

No joke.

You can put as little as $1 into the account—hey, every little bit helps.

The sooner in your life you start investing,
the richer you will be.

Here's something that'll blow your mind:

Every time I check the statistics it's different, but usually around half of Canadians who could open a TFSA (i.e., they're eighteen or older) have not done so.

THAT'S INSANE!

This is a chance for your money to grow and you don't have to pay tax on it!

WHY WOULD YOU NOT DO THIS?!?!?!

Here's why:

People. Don't. Know.

But you do. :)

The hammer exists. Use it.

P.S. As of this writing, in New Brunswick, Newfoundland and Labrador, Nova Scotia, Northwest Territories, Nunavut, Yukon, and B.C., you have to be nineteen years old to open a TFSA.

Why? Why is this the case? Why don't these provinces and territories just let people open TFSAs at eighteen like the other provinces?

I dunno…it's the system we live in.

I'll expand on this in the next chapter. Let's Level-up.

LEVEL-UP ON TFSAs

Golden Rule #3 is coming up, but first let's dive deeper into the TFSA.

Here are the nitty-gritty details so when you turn eighteen and walk into your bank, the banker will be like:

> "Whoa, holy crap! You really know your stuff!"

The TFSA is simply a doorway into the investing world. It's a way of getting your money there. It's a portal.

The TFSA itself is not an investment. As in, you can't just put money into a TFSA and think it's invested. It's not.

It has to go an extra step.

Think of it like walking through the front doors of a Walmart.

You walk into the store, that's step #1. But then you actually have to pick something and buy it. That's step #2.

It's the same thing here.

You put money into a TFSA. That's step #1. But then you actually have to buy something with it. That's step #2.

That's how you invest money.

Remember: *When you're investing, you're buying.*

> Future Millionaire: "Okay Doug, I put money into my TFSA. Now you're telling me I gotta buy something with it. So what can I buy?"
>
> Doug: "Anything: Stocks, bonds, mutual funds, ETFs, index funds, you name it!"
>
> Future Millionaire: "I'll assume you're planning on explaining all of those later in the book."
>
> Doug: "You would be correct."

The point I'm trying to make is it's no good simply putting money into your TFSA and being done with it.

Money won't grow if it sits in your account as "cash." It needs to go an extra step and actually be invested in something.

So how do you ensure your money gets invested in something?

Your bank will help you.

When you open your TFSA, your banker will ask you what you'd like to invest in. (At least, they're supposed to.)

They'll say something like, "You've put money into your TFSA—smart move. What would you like to invest it in?"

You should invest in things that interest you.

Remember, investing means you're buying pieces of companies and organizations, and they're gonna take your money and use it to help them grow.

So what companies do you wanna see grow?

Do you like green or sustainable energy? Ask the banker what options are available for investing in green energy.

Do you like groundbreaking technology? Robots, etc.? Ask the banker what the options are.

Do you like fashion or trends? What's available for investing in fashion?

There are so many different things you can invest in. Again, much more on this later.

Shifting gears. Here's a really great question:

> If TFSAs are so wonderful, why aren't they the *only* kind of account people use?

> Like, couldn't rich people just put millions of dollars into a TFSA, which would make them millions of more dollars, and it would all be tax-free?

Good news and bad news:

The bad news is there's a limit to how much money you're allowed to put into a TFSA.

The good news is the limit accumulates every year.

I'll explain.

The day you turn eighteen you can open a TFSA.

That particular year, whatever year it is, there will be a limit to how much money you can put into the account.

(If you google "what is the TFSA limit for ____ (insert year)," Google will tell you.)

Right now, it's 2024. If you turn eighteen this year, you're allowed to put up to $7,000 into a TFSA. No more. If you put in more, you'll get penalized—no good!

I know what you're thinking: "Doug, be real. How many eighteen-year-olds have $7,000 to put into a TFSA?!"

Totally. It's a lot of money, I get it.

But the goal should be to put in as much money as you can, each year, and try to max it out.

And by "max it out," I mean try to put as much in as you're allowed to. So if the limit is $7,000, aim to put in $7,000 throughout the year!

You might not get there, but that's okay because guess what? The contribution room rolls over into the next year.

So what does that mean?

First off, "contribution room" means the amount of money you're still allowed to deposit into your TFSA.

So if you turn eighteen today, your contribution room is $7,000.

Now, say your grandma writes you a cheque for $100 and you deposit all of it into your TFSA. (Smart move.)

As a result, your "contribution room" is now $6,900.

$$\$7,000 - \$100 = \$6,900$$

Got it?

Now, let's say you don't deposit any more money into your TFSA for the rest of the calendar year. (Not recommended, but fine.)

When January 1st rolls around, your new contribution room will be the $6,900 you already have PLUS the new year's TFSA limit.

For simplicity's sake, let's say the new year's limit is again $7,000.

That means as of January 1st, your new contribution room will be $6,900 + $7,000 = $13,900.

So in this new year, you can deposit up to $13,900 into your TFSA!

Make sense?

And let's say you waited until you were 20 years old before opening your first TFSA (again, not recommended).

Then your contribution room would be:

The limit from the year you turned 18 (let's say $7,000)

+

The limit from the year you turned 19 (let's say $7,000)

+

The limit from the year you turned 20 (let's say $7,000)

=

$21,000 in total

So by the time you turn 20, you can contribute up to $21,000.

(Again, assuming the government decides the limit is $7,000 for each of those years and assuming you hadn't opened a TFSA by that point. Which is, yet again, very much not recommended.)

At this point, I always get the following three questions from future millionaires.

Question #1

Future Millionaire: "So Doug, let's say I turn eighteen today. You're saying, because it's 2024, I'm allowed to put up to $7,000 into a TFSA, is that right?"

Doug: "You got it."

Future Millionaire: "If I only put $2,000 into the TFSA, that would mean I still have contribution room of $5,000, yes?"

Doug: "Bingo."

Future Millionaire: "But what if my $2,000 invested inside my TFSA makes me $500? Does that mean my contribution room goes from $5,000 down to $4,500?

In other words, does the money I make inside my TFSA count towards my contributions?"

Doug: "Great question. No. Only money from outside of the TFSA going *into* the TFSA counts as a contribution. All the money you make inside the TFSA does not count as a contribution."

Question #2

Future Millionaire: "What happens if I take money out of my TFSA? Am I allowed to put it back in?"

Doug: "As long as the total amount of money going *into* the TFSA does not exceed the allowable amount. If you've maxed it out, you gotta hang tight until January 1st."

Future Millionaire: "Um..."

I'll explain.

Let's say this year you manage to put a whopping $7,000 into your TFSA and max it out. That'd be awesome!

Now, for the rest of the year, you're not allowed to put any more money in.

(This makes sense, right? You "maxed it out." You put in the maximum you're allowed. You can't put anymore in.)

However, you can take out as much as you want, whenever you want.

You're just not allowed to put any more money in until the new year, until January 1st.

When January 1st arrives, you'll get the new limit, and then you can start making contributions again.

Now, let's say this year's limit is $7,000 and by mid-year you've managed to put in $4,000.

So you haven't maxed it out. You still have $3,000 of contribution room.

Again, you can take out as much as you want, but you're only allowed to put in up to $3,000 before the end of the year.

If you manage to put in $3,000 before the end of the year then your total contributions would be $4,000 + $3,000. And then your TFSA would be maxed out.

That's a tricky one. If you need to read that again, all good.

Here's something else to be aware of if you decide to take money out of your TFSA:

When January 1st rolls around, not only can you contribute up to the new limit, but *you can also put back the amount of money you took out!*

This is really awesome! Watch this:

Let's say you max out your TFSA with $7,000, and then in the same year, you decide to take out $3,000.

On January 1st, you can contribute up to the new year's limit (let's assume another $7,000) PLUS the $3,000 you took out.

So $10,000 in total.

It's almost like the money you take out becomes extra contribution room in the new year.

That's sweet!

Question #3

Future Millionaire: "I live in a province/territory where I have to be nineteen to open a TFSA...

(New Brunswick, Newfoundland and Labrador, Nova Scotia, Northwest Territories, Nunavut, Yukon, and B.C.)

...Does that mean I'll be a year behind the rest of the country?"

Doug: "Not necessarily, if you're smart. Listen closely:

If you live in one of the provinces/territories where you have to be nineteen to open a TFSA, *you still collect the contribution room from the year you turn eighteen.*"

Future Millionaire: "So...does that mean...when I turn 19, I can open a TFSA and put in double the amount of money?"

Doug: "Uh, sorta, ish."

Future Millionaire: "Or, to be more precise, I'll have two years' worth of contribution room when I turn nineteen and open the account."

Doug: "Exactly. So for example:

If you turn eighteen in 2024, this year's limit is $7,000.

Next year when you turn nineteen your contribution room will be this year's $7,000 plus whatever the new year's limit is.

If the new year's limit is another $7,000, then when you turn nineteen and open your TFSA you can contribute up to $14,000.

Make sense?"

Future Millionaire: "I think so…So the year I turn eighteen, even though I can't open a TFSA, maybe I could be saving money? Then I'll be prepared for the following year when I open my TFSA and have two years' worth of contribution room."

Doug: "Took the words right outta my mouth. Yes, 100%."

Throughout the year you turn eighteen, you can be saving up your money so you have a nice big chunk of change to contribute to your TFSA when you turn nineteen.

That would be brilliant. Like, really brilliant. Definitely do this.

So there we have it!

That, my friend, is GOLDEN RULE #2: MAX OUT YOUR TFSA.

You're doing awesome. Let's keep this ball rollin'.

Bring on Golden Rule #3.

GOLDEN RULE #3

SNOWBALL COMPOUND INTEREST

You ever made a snowman?

You know how when you roll the snowball it gets bigger and bigger?

In the Snowman World we call this "compound snow." In the Finance World we call this "compound interest."

Think of it like a ball of money that rolls into more money, which rolls into more money, etc.

Very important to understand if you wanna be a millionaire.

Remember, "interest" is a fancy word meaning "the extra money you make when you invest money."

So if you invest $100 and after a year, you have $108, your invested money made you $8 in interest.

This next sentence might sound obvious, but I'll say it anyway:

We describe the interest as a percentage of the amount of money invested.

So if you invested $100 and it made you $8 in interest, then:

$$8 \div 100 = 0.08 \ \text{ or } \ 8\%$$

You made 8% in interest.

(Yes, we're getting into some math. I know, I know. But this chapter ends with a million bucks, so stay with me.)

So you can now sound all fancy and say, "Yes, I earned an annual interest rate of 8% on my $100."

You're pretty much ready for Wall Street.

I'll mention that 8% is a good interest rate. It could be higher, it could be lower, but we'll go with 8% for this example.

Now, if you made 8% on your $100, and at the end of the year you took your $8 out of the account and spent it, you would still have your original $100 invested.

Which means next year you might make another $8 in interest, which you could also take out and go spend.

So each year you're making $8. You're then taking it out of the account and you're spending it. Fine.

But what would happen if you didn't take it out? What would happen if you just left that $8 in the account?

If you just leave it in there, things start to get real interesting real fast.

Check it out:

End of Year 1: You earn 8% on $100. You now have $108. *You keep the money in the account.*

End of Year 2: You earn 8% on $108. You now have $116.64. *You keep the money in there.*

End of Year 3: You earn 8% on $116.64. You now have $125.97. *Keep it in there.*

You get the idea. Let's fast-forward.

End of Year 20: You earn 8% on $431.57. You now have $466.10.

So you invested $100, and after twenty years your money grew to $466.10.

It compounded. (Hence "compound interest.")

Meaning your invested money made you more money, which made you more money, which made you more money, etc.

You invested $100, you didn't touch it, and miraculously it grew to become $466.10 all by itself! That's incredible!

Okay, okay, okay, I know what you're thinking:

"Doug, who cares?! I started with $100 and I have to wait *TWENTY YEARS* and it only gets me $466.10?! Big deal!"

Fair enough.

Buuuuuuuuut, let's say each year, you put in another $100.

So each year the account would earn 8% plus an extra $100 from you.

Check it out (and hold on to your socks!):

End of Year 1: You earn 8% on $100. You now have $108. *You add $100. New total: $208.*

End of Year 2: You earn 8% on $208. You now have $224.64. *You add $100. Total: $324.64.*

End of Year 3: You earn 8% on $324.64. You now have $350.61. *You add $100. Total: $450.61.*

You get it. Fast-forward.

End of Year 20: You earn 8% on $4,576.20. You now have $4,942.29. You add $100.

FINAL TOTAL: $5,042.29

In total you contributed $2,100.

But the account is worth $5,042.29! Out of thin air you've made almost $3,000!!!

That's more than your total contributions of $2,100!

Love. It.

Okay, now this is getting exciting. Let's say you did it with $1,000 instead of $100.

Now, a thousand bucks might sound like a lot, but it's only $2.74 a day for a year. Think you could do it?

If you could save $2.74 a day, you'd be able to contribute $1,000 to your account every year. And here's what would happen (again, assuming 8% interest):

End of Year 1: You earn 8% on $1,000. You now have $1,080. *You add $1,000. Total: $2,080.*

End of Year 2: You earn 8% on $2,080. You now have $2,246.40. *Add $1,000. Total: $3,246.40.*

Fast-forward.

End of Year 20: You've contributed $20,000, but your new total is...

$50,422.92!!!!! WHAT!?!?!?!?

Let's take it a step further. You ready?

Remember how we talked about the TFSA and how each year you're allowed to put a certain amount of money into it?

Well, the amount you're allowed to put into a TFSA has never been less than $5,000/year.

So let's use $5,000 and 8% and see what happens.

End of Year 1: You earn 8% on $5,000. You now have $5,400. *You add $5,000. New total: $10,400.*

End of Year 2: You earn 8% on $10,400. You now have $11,232. *You add $5,000.*

Fast-forward.

End of Year 37: The total amount of money you invested is $185,000, but the total amount of money you have is...

$1,101,579.73

Millionaire. Boom.

You did it.

Now, does investing $5,000 a year sound unrealistic?

It's only $13.70 a day. The current hourly minimum wage in Ontario is $16.55 (as of 2024).

Which means at a minimum wage job where you're investing *less than one hour's pay a day*, you could retire as a millionaire by age fifty-four.

That's *eleven years* earlier than the standard retirement age of sixty-five.

You wanna be a millionaire at some point in your life? Don't buy a lottery ticket; use your smarts!

You can do it! It is 100% possible.

It just takes brains, discipline, and time.

And compound interest, of course.

There's the pathway. Walk it.

YOUR PARENTS #1

So get this:

By the end of this book, it's very possible you're gonna know more about money than your parents do.

I mean that with no disrespect to your parents—they might agree!

It could be really interesting to have a (gentle) conversation with them about the THREE GOLDEN RULES.

Have they ever considered the idea of "paying yourself first"?

Have they opened a TFSA? Do they know how the TFSA works?

Are they taking advantage of compound interest through their investments?

Be gentle with them, okay? People get very sensitive when talking about money.

Remember, if they don't know about this stuff, it's okay! It's not their fault.

Try to keep it casual:

"Hey Mom, I'm reading this book and it's talking about Tax-Free Savings Accounts? They sound pretty great. What do you think of them?"

"Hey Dad, in my book the author is talking about the pay-yourself-first rule by investing 10% of your income. What do you think? Have you ever experimented with that?"

Look, the world of money can be intimidating and scary.

People have a tendency to shy away from it because it can make them feel stupid.

It made me feel stupid. (Hell, it still makes me feel stupid.)

And *nobody* likes that feeling. *Nobody.*

So if your parents don't know much about this stuff, *it's all good.* I totally and completely understand.

Or, hey, maybe your parents are bankers or accountants or something, and they know way more about this stuff than I do.

If so, awesome.

All the more reason to have a conversation with them.

THE GOLDEN RECAP

Back to you.

Hey, it's page 55! I haven't forgotten the deal we made. You held up your end of the bargain—nice work!

If you stop reading now and don't go any further, I'll still feel I've done my job.

If you apply the THREE GOLDEN RULES, starting at your age, you will be unstoppable.

- PAY YOURSELF 10% FIRST
- MAX OUT YOUR TFSA
- SNOWBALL COMPOUND INTEREST (i.e. Don't take money out of the account once invested.)

If you seriously do this and you're diligent, it is my belief that you will be a millionaire at some point in your life. And you will retire early.

I've shown you the hammers. Nail that sucker home.

So, I know what you're thinking:

"Doug, if I now understand the pathway to becoming a millionaire, why would I keep reading?"

Good question. Let me ask you something:

How fast do you wanna get there?

CHUNK 2
THE SKI SLOPE

FASTER OR SLOWER

Have you ever been downhill skiing? It's fun.

I mean, who wouldn't wanna strap laminated wood to their feet and hurl themselves down the side of a mountain?

But seriously. Good times.

When I was a kid, I'd make it my personal goal to go from the top of the ski hill to the bottom as fast as humanly possible.

The steeper the slope, the faster I'd go. Epic.

But here's what I quickly realized:

The steeper slope meant I'd go faster, but it also meant a much higher possibility of a full-on yard-sale wipeout.

(Which is when you fall and all the equipment attached to you comes flying off and scatters across the ski slope.)

Ouch.

Steeper slope = Faster time = Higher risk

I'll bring this all back to becoming a millionaire in a second, I promise.

In skiing, you have three different ski slope difficulty levels. All of them will get you to your destination (the bottom of the hill), but in different ways.

The Green Circle - The nice 'n easy, gentle slope. Very little chance of wiping out. You'll get to the bottom slowly and safely.

The Blue Square - The middle one. A bit faster and more challenging than the green circle. You could wipe out, but it's not likely if you've got some experience.

The Black Diamond - The steep one. Fast, risky. More dangerous. Your chances of a wipeout are much greater, but you could also get to the bottom a lot faster if you don't fall.

They'll all get you to the bottom of the hill, but they all have different levels of risk.

It's the same when you invest money.

Getting to millionaire status is like getting to the bottom of the ski hill. How are you gonna get there? Faster with more risk? Or slower and more safely?

There's no "right" answer. There's no one perfect way. It all comes down to how you feel.

Do you wanna play it safe? Or are you someone who is comfortable with a bit of risk?

Are you a Green Circle? Blue Square? Or Black Diamond? Again, no "right" answer.

Whichever ski slope you decide will determine what kinds of things you invest in through your Tax-Free Savings Account.

But before we dive into each slope in detail, let's talk about the entire ski hill: The stock market.

IN A NUTSHELL:

THE STOCK MARKET
(THE ENTIRE SKI HILL)

The terms "stock market" and "stock exchange" are often used interchangeably.

But technically, "stock market" is the broader, generic term.

So I could say, "The stock market is the place to buy stocks and bonds."

While "stock exchange" is more specific, often to location.

> "Hey, can you tell me on which stock exchange I can buy stock in the company 'Pinterest'?"

> "Sure, you can buy Pinterest stock on the New York Stock Exchange."

In Canada there are several stock exchanges, the largest being the Toronto Stock Exchange, also known as the "TSX."

In the United States there are two really big ones:

1) The New York Stock Exchange
2) The Nasdaq (which stands for National Association of Securities Dealers something something...I forget. Google it if you're interested.)

So what exactly is a stock exchange?

It's literally the "market place" for buying and selling financial securities.

"Financial securities" are stocks, bonds, etc. Fancy pieces of paper representing a tiny portion of something, like a company for instance.

It's the slice of the pie.

Most of the stock market has gone digital; the actual pieces of paper are a thing of the past.

Here's the thing: People get wildly rich using the stock market and the different exchanges.

At stock exchanges, people watch the prices of financial securities go up and down, up and down, all day long.

The prices fluctuate based on "supply and demand."

I know it sounds dull, but that's what it is. People selling vs. people buying.

When tons of people are trying to sell and not many people wanna buy, prices go down.

When tons of people are trying to buy and not many people wanna sell, prices go up.

In the next few chapters, we're gonna chat about some of the different financial securities you can invest in on the stock market.

Specifically bonds, funds, and stocks, in that order.

This is where we'll apply the whole Green Circle, Blue Square, Black Diamond thing we talked about.

In general, I want you to think of it like this:

Bonds — Green Circle (Easy)

Funds — Blue Square (Medium)

Stocks — Black Diamond (Difficult)

Again, this is a *general* way of thinking about this.

Now, you remember how investing is buying? (You put money into your TFSA, but then you actually gotta *buy something* with it.)

Well, now you'll have some options. Will you buy bonds? Will you buy funds? Or will you buy stocks?

It will all depend on your comfort level with the different degrees of risk. Slower and safer? Or faster and riskier?

We're gonna dive into all three—bonds, funds, and stocks—to build your understanding of each one so you can make decisions that will be best for you.

You ready to go? Hop on the chairlift.

Let's ski some slopes.

IN A NUTSHELL:

BONDS (GREEN CIRCLE)

In general, bonds are the safe and slow investment. The Green Circle ski slope.

A bond is someone else's debt that you buy. You lend them money and they promise to pay you back at an established time in the future with a prearranged interest rate...

Hmmm. That's confusing. Okay, let me try another way.

When I was a kid, I would save loonies by putting them in a loonie jar.

My older sister would sometimes want to borrow a few of said loonies.

Being the considerate younger brother that I am, I was prepared to lend her a few loonies, but I also wanted to get something out of this deal.

And I needed proof she would *actually pay those loonies back.*

So we devised a system where she would borrow ten loonies right now, in the present.

But then, in exactly one month, she would pay me back eleven loonies; the ten she owed me, plus an extra one.

This sounded great!

All I had to do was lend her the money, and in a month I'd have my ten loonies back plus an extra one.

Sweet!

But I still needed proof. I needed a contract. I love my sister, but this was a whopping *ten loonies* I was dishing out.

So she agreed to give me an "IOU." She wrote on a piece of paper, "In one month, I owe you 11 loonies."

Perfect. We had a contract. I was gonna make money here. Excellent!

The evil villain in my five-year-old self cackled with glee. I had her signature in blood. (Okay, not in blood. But you get what I mean.)

We were bonded.

A bond is an IOU.

Here's how it works with a lemonade stand:

Let's say you're six years old and you wanna sell lemonade. You need lemons, sugar, cups, a sign, and chalk.

You currently don't have any of those things. You need to buy them.

You add up the cost of each item and realize you need $20 in total just to get started.

But you don't have any money. You haven't sold any lemonade yet! How are you gonna do this?

So you decide to go door-to-door until you find four adults in the neighbourhood who are each willing to lend you $5.

And in return for the $5, you give each of the adults a piece of paper that says this:

> Dear Adult,
>
> In a week, after I make money selling lemonade, I promise I will give you back your $5. Plus, I will give you an extra dollar to say "thanks for investing in me." So in a week I will give you $6 altogether.
>
> Sincerely, Young Future Millionaire

Everyone wins.

You win because you get the money to start your lemonade stand.

The neighbourhood wins because who doesn't like lemonade?

And the four adults win because they all know in a week they'll get their money back, plus an extra dollar.

You have "issued them a bond." They are now "bond holders."

And finally, here's how it works on a much bigger scale.

Say your city's government wants to build a new sports stadium. The cost of the stadium might be much more than the city's government can afford.

But the government also knows that once the stadium is built, it will bring in tons of money selling tickets, hot dogs, drinks, etc.

The government wants to borrow money right now, believing they will profit in the future.

So they ask the people of the city to pitch in some money, and in return the government will give them an IOU (a bond).

Also, the city is not asking people to lend out of the goodness of their hearts. No, no.

The city offers to pay interest (the little bit extra).

So the government says to the people:

> "Hello people of the city! We want to build a stadium of epic proportions, but we need money to do it.
>
> If you will lend us your money, buy our bonds, we promise to pay you back in five years' time. Plus, we will pay you 5% more of whatever you lend us."

The people who agree to lend the money (or "buy the bond") are now the bond holders.

If you buy a bond, you know in five years you'll have been paid back the money, plus 5% of whatever you lent.

Bonds are typically low-risk—Green Circle—because you know the time frame and the predetermined interest rate.

Government bonds are probably the safest of all.

Bonds can be higher risk if it's questionable whether the organization borrowing the money will actually be able to pay it back.

Like with the lemonade stand, can the four adults trust you to be able to pay back their original $5 plus the extra $1 you're promising?

What if you set up the lemonade stand, and nobody buys any lemonade?

You won't make any money which means you won't be able to pay back the four adults.

This is a risk everyone takes. The four adults recognize they could lose their $5 completely.

And maybe, for the four adults, the $5 risk isn't worth the extra $1 they'll make.

If that's the case, maybe you need to sweeten the deal and offer them a return of $1.50 instead of only $1.

Usually the higher the questionability, the higher the interest rate.

In other words, if it's a higher risk for the bond buyer, it should come with a higher reward.

In the example with my sister, I let her borrow ten loonies and she had to pay me back eleven.

That's a 10% interest rate. That's pretty high for a bond.

Which would indicate that even as a five-year-old, handing loonies over to my sister, I was questioning my chances of ever seeing them again.

If she borrowed ten and gave me back eleven—success!

If she borrowed ten and never returned any...

Huh.

...I need to make a phone call...

IN A NUTSHELL:

FUNDS (BLUE SQUARE)

Do you like Timbits?

I definitely do. Especially the assorted-flavour boxes.

When I walk into Tim Hortons, instead of buying the entire chocolate donut or the entire honey dip donut, I want the Timbits.

I want a little piece of all of them.

In the investing world, instead of investing all your money in one or two big companies, you can buy a little box with tiny pieces of a bunch of different companies.

Like Timbits.

This is great for people like me who want a tiny taste of all of them. Investing in a "fund" allows you to do this.

And you know how at Tim Hortons there's someone who puts the Timbits into the box before handing it to you?

In the investing world, there are organizations that do the same thing. They pick out which companies to put inside the box.

They are known as "fund companies."

They take the empty Timbit box. They decide which pieces of other companies should go inside. Then they sell it to you as a single package.

But instead of the package being called a "Timbit box," it's called a "share."

So if someone buys 100 shares from a fund company, then what they're buying is 100 identical Timbit boxes each with the exact same ratio of flavours/companies inside.

But hang on.

What if you don't like some of the companies inside the box? Or you'd prefer others?

This is why a there are hundreds of funds!

So you get to shop around to find the one you like.

It's like you're allowed to dig through different Timbit boxes to find the one with your favourite ratio of flavours (the one with the most chocolate, obviously).

And because you're investing in all the companies inside the box, this means you're "diversifying" your investments.

Which is fancy talk for "investing in more than one company."

Smart move.

So if one company plummets to $0, you still have the others.

Before funds came into existence, if you wanted to invest in different companies, you had to buy stocks in each company individually, one at a time.

That took a lot of work!

People wanna invest, but they don't wanna work that hard! And who can blame them?

Investing in companies one at a time requires reading and research, which only nerds like me wanna do.

But now we have funds!

And funds are awesome because they're a one-stop shop to diversify your investments.

Instead of buying one or two companies, you're buying tiny morsels of a whole bunch of them. Like Timbits.

So that's the basic idea. But there are different types of funds; different categories:

1) Mutual funds

2) Index funds

3) Exchange-traded funds (ETFs)

We'll dive into each and put the "fun" into "funds"…

Dad joke, sorry.

Back on the chairlift. Let's tackle the Blue Square slopes.

(P.S. I rewrote this chapter six times. And after each time, I had to go to Tim Hortons to get Timbits. Not even joking.)

IN A NUTSHELL:

MUTUAL FUNDS (BLUE SQUARE)

You know the saying "Safety in numbers"? Like, if you're part of a group, you're safer?

Basically, that's a mutual fund.

When you buy shares of a mutual fund, you become part of a huge group of people who have decided to pool their money together and leave it with a "mutual fund company."

The people are like:

> "Hey, mutual fund company, here's our money. You decide which Timbit combination you think is best, which group of companies to invest in…
>
> …You do the work and make us rich! We'd do it ourselves, but we have lives to live."

The mutual fund company has (hopefully) expert fund managers who try to make smart decisions about what to do with the money—which companies to invest in.

> *They decide which Timbits to put inside the box.*

Mutual funds are known as "actively managed" investments.

Which is a fancy way of saying "expert people—fund managers—are working to try to make you rich."

But these fund managers don't work for free.

There's always a fee for being part of a mutual fund.

The fee is usually a percentage of the money that you (the client) have invested with the mutual fund company.

Let's say you invest $100 and they charge a 2% fee.

That means they'll take $2 from the money that's made from the investment.

If your $100 grows by 7% (meaning your money made you $7), the mutual fund company takes $2. And you get $5.

Make sense?

Also, they might charge a percentage of the money that is earned from the investment. Which would incentivize them to work harder.

Think about it:

If the fund managers know they'll make a portion of the money that's earned, they're going to work as hard as they can to make as much as possible.

And that means more money for you! Excellent.

But can I tell you something ridiculous about the fee?

Instead of just calling it a "mutual fund fee," they decided to come up with really, really dumb name for it.

They call it the "Management Expense Ratio."

slaps forehead

Seriously?! At least it gets shortened to "MER." But still.

So if you're browsing mutual fund info (and who isn't?), and you see 'MER', you'll know that's the fee.

And it will likely be in the range of 1 - 3%.

Another thing you might see is "YTD," which stands for "year to date."

This tells us how well the mutual fund has performed since January 1st.

In other words, how much bigger have all the Timbits inside the box gotten, on average, since the start of the year?

Maybe they've grown by 1%? Or 2%? Or maybe more like 7 or 8%?

It's always good to have an idea of how well they're growing.

Also, here's a fact: The price of a mutual fund is updated only once a day, after the stock markets close.

Is that the most boring mutual fund fact I could tell you?

Yes.

But it's important to mention because it's one of the key differences between mutual funds and exchange-traded funds (coming up in two chapters).

So if you wanna know the updated price of a mutual fund, you gotta wait until the end of the work day.

You can google "most popular mutual funds in Canada" and there'll be tons of information.

The whole process of investing in a mutual fund can be summed up in six steps:

1) You pool your money with other investors.
2) You leave it with a mutual fund company.
3) The company makes decisions on how to invest it.
4) They make you (and all the other investors) money.
5) They take a tiny slice.
6) You're left with the rest.

It's a pretty good deal.

Mutual funds are popular because they're usually pretty safe, but they usually "yield high returns."

Which is investment slang for "make you pretty good money."

Of course, just like skiing down a Blue Square slope, you can still wipe out.

But in general, you'll probably be okay.

And lots of people don't mind paying a fee if they know they've got expert fund managers actively working for them to make them rich.

On the flip side, there are lots of people who don't wanna pay a fee for a complete stranger, who calls themselves an "expert," to manage their money.

Fair enough.

People who feel this way might prefer a more "passively managed" investment.

This means instead of paying someone to design a custom-built Timbit box (which is what a mutual fund is), they'd prefer a pre-existing Timbit box that no one manages and therefore has almost no fee.

For those people, there's a great option:

The index fund.

IN A NUTSHELL:

INDEX FUNDS (BLUE SQUARE)

An index fund is a pre-existing Timbit box.

You buy it the way it is. It doesn't get customized for you, and you don't get to choose the companies inside the box.

But it has very, very low fees because nobody is managing it.

And maybe you're okay with that if you believe the companies inside the box are already great companies.

For instance, what if I told you that you could buy a Timbit box full of tiny pieces of the 500 largest companies in the U.S.?

It would be like me saying, "So you can't customize it, but here's a Timbit box with the 500 most popular flavours."

Sounds pretty good right?

It's real.

It's called the "S&P 500 Index" and it's a fund that invests in the largest 500 publicly traded companies in the U.S.

"Publicly traded" just means you and I, the public, can invest in them.

(And "S&P" stands for "Standard & Poor's." Not that you need to know that, but whatever. Now you do.)

If you invest a single dollar with the S&P 500 Index Fund, your dollar gets divided up into 500 tiny pieces, and each company gets a piece.

Some of the companies will grow a lot, and some of them might not grow at all, but you will be right in the middle.

The average of all of them.

And the average growth of the top 500 companies in the U.S is *likely* gonna be pretty good.

So very low fees, very little work, and a relatively high chance of a decent return (i.e. you'll probably make good money).

This is another great choice for people who want the Blue Square ski slope.

Assuming those 500 huge companies continue to make money, you will too.

If this sounds good to you, say this to your banker:

> "I'd like to invest in index funds inside my TFSA. Can you suggest a few I might be interested in? Perhaps the S&P 500 Index? Or the S&P/TSX 60 Index?"

See what they say. And have them describe the fund to you so you understand.

Index funds are simply the average of a bunch of companies.

No one is working for you. You buy an index fund, and you accept the average.

And that's certainly not a bad thing.

After all, being right in the middle means you're always doing better than 50% of the market.

Glass half full.

Now if you're thinking, "Okay, this sounds good, but maybe I'm interested in doing better than the middle, and I'm okay with a bit of risk, but I'm not quite ready for a Black Diamond."

Well, my friend, I have the answer:

Exchange-traded funds.

IN A NUTSHELL:

EXCHANGE-TRADED FUNDS
(BLUE SQUARE)

You want a bit more excitement?

Exchange-traded funds (ETFs) might be the answer. They're sort of a combination of index and mutual funds.

(I'll try to make this quick. I'm aware this is the *fourth* chapter on funds.)

Here's how an ETF works:

A whole bunch of people pool their money together, then a fund manager decides what to invest it in.

Wait a sec. This sounds like a mutual fund, right?

But here's the difference:

Remember how with a mutual fund, the price gets updated only once a day? (After the stock markets close.)

It's not the same with an ETF.

Instead, the price of an ETF can change on a minute-by-minute basis.

So just like the price of a stock; the price goes up and down, up and down, all day long.

Fun Fact: With ETFs there's often a theme.

For instance, maybe an ETF is invested only in green-energy investments.

So if you're like me and you like green energy, maybe you'd be interested in that ETF.

These days, more young people are choosing to invest in ETFs. Why is that?

I think it's because ETF's tend to be more exciting to trade (like stocks of a company), but they're relatively safe and diversified.

And by having themes, ETFs allow investors to quickly and easily identify funds that align with their own values.

So there we go. That's it!

I promised I'd try to make it quick. Hopefully it wasn't too painful.

And hopefully you've got a good handle on these things now.

But if you don't, don't worry. The point is just to start thinking about it. You don't have to become a master of funds.

(Although, if you do become a master, call me, I have more questions.)

Future Millionaire: "Hold up, Doug. What's the difference between mutual funds and ETFs?…

…You said the price of a mutual fund gets updated once a day and the price of an ETF gets updated once a minute. Any other differences?"

Doug: "Honestly, not really."

They're very similar. I probably could've squished them together into the same chapter.

The only thing is, in the investing world, they both get talked about so frequently, I wanted to highlight both of them.

P.S. At this point, I wanna mention Socially Responsible Investment Funds (SRIFs).

SRIFs are Timbit boxes filled with companies that have been carefully selected based on environmental, social, and governance criteria.

I'm mentioning them because they're becoming particularly popular among young people.

If this interests you, you can definitely invest in these through your Tax-Free Savings Account. Talk to your banker about this.

I just recommend doing more research to make sure they're a good fit for you.

IN A NUTSHELL:

STOCKS (BLACK DIAMOND)

People said to me, "Doug, they're seventeen. They're too young to learn about stocks."

I disagreed.

And yet, I almost deleted this chapter.

Loads of people reminded me of the reputation teenagers have for poor decision-making and pointed out that stocks are very risky—*Black Diamond*.

So I ask you: Are you ready?

You've made it this far in the book—huge congratulations by the way!—I'm guessing you can probably handle this.

But if I'm wrong, simply skip this chapter. All good.

…

Hangin' in there? Cool.

Here comes a basic foundation in stocks. But I'll still caution you, as I would anybody, regardless of their age.

CAUTION: STOCKS ARE HIGH-RISK.

THE MOST YOU CAN LOSE IS EVERYTHING.

Sorry to scare you, but it's important to say that.

Okay, here we go.

As we've discussed before, if a company is like a giant pie, a stock is a very tiny slice.

A company sells stocks to investors in order to raise money.

The company says, "Okay, we need money to expand the business…

…Why don't we sell tiny pieces of ownership to people, which will make us a bunch of money to help us grow?"

And that's exactly what happens.

Think of it in five steps:

1) The company divides itself into many tiny slices (stocks).

2) Investors (you and I) buy the stock.

3) The company uses the money to expand the business.

4) The company becomes more valuable over time (and ideally, the price of the stock goes up).

5) You and I sell the stock for more than we bought it for and we make money.

You can buy stocks through your TFSA or any investing account.

Remember, stocks are the Black Diamond ski slope:

Potentially fast but risky.

You have a higher chance of making lots of money, but you also have a higher chance of wiping out (i.e. losing money).

With stocks, you must do your research. And you must exercise patience.

Research. Patience. Research. Patience.

Am I getting the message across?

I think you'd agree it would be foolish to tackle a Black Diamond ski slope without some skiing experience.

The "experience" is the research. Never buy a stock without doing your research. Ever.

There are two kinds of people when it comes to stocks: "Traders" and "Investors."

Traders are people who try all day long to profit off the minute-by-minute rises and falls of the stock market.

Some days they win, some days they lose.

Investors are people who research companies, pick the ones they believe in, buy the stock, then sit back, relax, and watch it increase in value over time.

Then years later, investors sell their stock for a much higher price and make tons of money.

My advice? Be an investor.

Unless, of course, you wanna spend your day watching the markets go up and down, up and down…hey, lots of people do, no judgement.

For most of us, being an investor is the way to go. It's simple and straightforward. Check out the process:

Research > Buy > Sit back > Relax > Wait > Sell > Get rich

Sweet, right?

You're like, "Okay, I'll be an investor. So what kind of research do I have to do?"

First off, what are you interested in? You should invest in companies that sell products or services you like!

Back to Coca-Cola. Do you drink it? Doesn't matter.

If you google "Coca-Cola stock," all the information about the stock and the company will pop up (pun intended). Try it with a different company, ideally one you like.

Then dive deeper.

Read about the company. Read about their CEO (big boss). Read about their mission.

Why do they exist? What are they trying to accomplish? How are they doing it?

Could you explain it to a five-year-old? And would they understand?

(FYI: If you can't explain what a company does in a way that a 5-year-old would understand, and yet you're considering buying some of their stock, I'd proceed cautiously.)

Do you feel "aligned with the company's values"? As in, do you feel you "connect with the company"?

Are you excited about their products or services?

Are other people also excited? What are the customer reviews saying?

Is the company successful?

Once you've done your research—and ONLY once you've done your research—if you see potential in the company, you can buy some of their stock.

This can be done through your TFSA.

You can ask your banker how to do this when you open your TFSA. It's not hard but get them to show you how. It can be done online.

Decide on a time horizon.

How long are you gonna hold the stock for before you sell it and make tons of money? Three years? Five years? Longer?

(FYI: Usually the longer you hold the stock, the richer you'll be when you sell it.)

And then…sit back, relax, and wait.

Pretty simple strategy, right? And it should be. Because y'know what? When investing in stocks, simpler = smarter.

I'm almost certain Warren Buffet would agree with me, and he's like, the guru of investing.

Quick recap:

    Bonds — Green Circle, Low-risk.

    Funds — Blue Square, Medium-risk.

    Stocks — Black Diamond, High-risk.

And there we have it! The ski slope analogy is complete. Nice job on the slopes! (Seriously, though, you're doing great.)

Warm chalet and hot chocolate, anyone?

P.S. A few of our test readers (the ones who are avid skiers) asked me if there was a "Double Black Diamond."

As in, an investment or strategy they should absolutely, 100% stay away from.

I thought about this for a while and have concluded two things:

1) If you buy a stock without having done your research, I'd consider that Double Black Diamond. Or maybe just idiotic. Like going from the bunny hill directly to a Black Diamond. Don't be stupid.

2) I'd also consider "shorting a stock" to be Double Black Diamond.

"Shorting a stock" is when you borrow a stock from someone (i.e. it doesn't belong to you), then you sell it and hope it drops in value. As in, you hope the price falls.

If the price does indeed fall, you can buy back the stock at a cheaper price and then return it to its original owner while you keep the difference.

Basically, it's a way to make money if you think a stock price will drop.

It's very, VERY risky because there's no limit to how much money you can lose.

Like, not only can you lose all your money and end up with $0, but it can get even worse; you can go into an infinite amount of debt.

I don't short stocks. I'll never short a stock.

I don't mind a bit of risk, but voluntarily skiing off the edge of a cliff isn't for me.

A NOTE ABOUT

INVESTING IN STOCKS

I thought I'd add this chapter because it's a valuable bit of info.

Usually, the longer the time horizon for holding a stock, the lower the risk.

Even if you buy stock in Tesla (currently considered by many to be very high-risk), if you plan on hanging on to it for five to ten years or longer, you'll minimize the risk.

How?

Because chances are the stock will generally trend upwards over time.

So the longer you hold on to it, the more likely you'll see higher returns averaged out over the long run.

In other words, don't worry about a stock's day-to-day price changes (which might resemble a rollercoaster). Instead, step back and look at how it's performed over the years.

If the company has been smart and had good leadership, the stock price has probably climbed over time.

But here's the key point: *It takes time.*

This is why it is *so* important to start this stuff the moment you turn eighteen. It can't be overstated.

I sound like a broken record here, but I promise you:

> *When you turn eighteen, if you start investing,*
> *even just a little bit, it will be one of the greatest*
> *decisions you make in your entire life.*

I realize that's a pretty bold statement. What do you think? Too bold?

Hand me a megaphone.

DOUG'S DEFAULT INVESTMENT PLAN

Quick check-in. How're you doin'? You good?

Are you thinking, "Bonds? Funds? Stocks? I dunno Doug, just tell me what to do!"

If you're feeling like that, all good. I gotcha.

I thought I'd include a default Quick-Start plan of action (like the Quick-Start button on a treadmill—love that button).

This chapter is if you wanna start investing but you're not sure how you feel about the different levels of risk.

This plan of action will help you get going, and it's relatively easy and painless.

Note: This is not advice. *It's a suggestion.*

At your meeting when you open your TFSA, tell the banker you'd like to "diversify your investments between a Canadian index fund and a global index fund."

This means you'll be investing in 1) the Canadian economy and 2) the global economy.

In other words, you're investing in the likelihood that companies in both Canada and around the world will continue to sell products and services.

And people in Canada and around the world will continue to buy them.

Do you think there's a good chance of that happening? If so, this is a great default option.

Why Canadian and global?

I suggest Canadian and global index funds because I believe it's important to invest in our own country's products and services, but I also think the rest of the world has a lot to offer.

This allows us to invest in both.

Doing this will be relatively low-risk; somewhere between Green Circle and Blue Square.

Pretty safe. Pretty secure. Pretty good returns.

Excellent default.

DOLLAR-COST AVERAGING

Okay, this is super cool.

Or at least, I think it is. Maybe that's me being a total nerd. But seriously, it's cool.

First of all, here's what you gotta know: People get scared when the market dips.

If they see stock prices falling, they go nuts.

It's probably not their fault if they were never taught, but they let their emotions run wild:

> "Oh crap, the market is going down!
> I'm gonna lose all my money! Sell! Sell! Sell!"

They get scared. Emotions take over. And then they sell when the value of their securities (stocks/bonds/funds, etc.) has gone down.

This is not smart. This is the opposite of smart. This is very stupid.

Because a few days later, the market will *probably* rebound and go back up.

"Oh crap, it's back up! Buy! Buy! Buy!"

So they sold at a low price and bought at a high price. No good.

When people do this, when they "panic sell" — and millions of people do it — it's a sign they are not confident in what they're invested in.

They don't trust their investment choices.

They got insecurities about their securities.

(Ooh! That's good. Can I trademark that?...)

Anyway, if they've been smart, if they've done their research and believe the bond/fund/stock they're invested in is a solid investment, then a dip in the market shouldn't be seen as a setback, but as an opportunity.

It's like a big blowout sale at their favourite store!

"ALL ITEMS 25% - 40% OFF! FOR A LIMITED TIME ONLY! EVERYTHING MUST GO!"

If you've done the research, if you're confident in your investment choices, then buy more!

It's on sale!

Okay, okay, okay, I know what you're thinking:

"But Doug, that means I have to be watching the market every day, constantly checking the prices. I can't be bothered, I'm bored already, I'm seventeen, I have a life to live."

Yeah, fair enough.

So now I introduce to you…drum roll please…

"Dollar-cost averaging."

Angelic choir sounds

Here's how it works:

You make regular lump-sum payments to your investments at regular intervals regardless of the market.

I'll explain.

Let's say you own shares of a fund through one of your investment accounts (like your TFSA).

To take advantage of dollar-cost averaging, you would add, for instance, $100 every month.

MONTH#	Month 1	Month 2	Month 3
$/month	$100	$100	$100

And let's say in Month 1 the shares of the fund are selling for $1 each. So your $100 buys you 100 shares.

Sweet.

Ready for a bit more math? Sorry, not sorry.

So now you own 100 shares and the Total Value of those shares is $100. (Pay close attention to the 'Total Value.' That's important.)

In Month 1 the Total Value = $100

But then in Month 2 there's a dip. The share price falls to $0.80. ("Oh crap! It's going down!")

You don't panic. You ignore everyone else who is panicking.

You stick to the plan. Because you've done your research and you're confident in what you've invested in.

You add another $100 to the investments.

But now, because of the dip, your $100 buys you 125 shares at a price of $0.80 each.

So for Month 2:

Total amount invested = $200

Total amount of shares purchased = 225

Total Value = $180

"Hold up, Doug. How did you get a Total Value of $180?"

Good question. Let's clarify.

By the end of Month 2, you own 225 shares. Because of the dip, each share is now worth $0.80.

$$225 \times \$0.80 = \$180$$

So yes, at the moment this kinda sucks. We've invested $200, but the Total Value is only $180.

We've lost some money. Now is when most people panic-sell, and lose even more.

But not you. Again, assuming you've done your research and you're confident.

Because watch what happens:

In Month 3, the market comes out of the dip and the price of the shares returns to $1.

You're sticking to your plan, so you invest another $100, which buys you another 100 shares at $1 each.

So now for Month 3:

Total amount invested = $300

Total amount of shares purchased = 325

Total Value = $325

We're up $25! And the stock hasn't even increased in value from its original price of $1!

While everyone else was panicking, you made a return of 8%! In only three months!

Many investments don't do that well in an *entire year,* and you just did it in ninety days!

Mind. Blown.

And here's the best part! ("We're not even at the best part yet?!" I know, it's epic.)

You can set this up to be automated with your bank so you never have to think about it. Like, ever.

It's called a "Regular Investment Plan."

You tell the bank how often you want to make the deposits (weekly, monthly, etc.) and then it just happens.

When you walk into the bank, say this:

"Hi, I'd like to set up a Regular Investment Plan through my TFSA to take advantage of dollar-cost averaging."

And they'll be like, "You're a financial genius."

You're welcome.

IN A NUTSHELL:

DIVIDENDS

Excellent. I've been looking forward to this chapter.

I love dividends.

And I think you will too once I explain them.

A dividend is a thank you card with a cheque inside that gets mailed to you every three to four months.

(i.e., a dividend is money.)

Do you drink Coca-Cola? Have I asked you this already? Doesn't matter.

Let's say you decide to invest in Coca-Cola, so you buy some stock and hope the company does well.

Coca-Cola continues selling its beverages, does *extremely* well, and makes a massive amount of money.

Now the company has some options.

They could put all that money into expanding the business, building factories, advertising, etc.

OR...

They can divide the money up amongst their investors, all the people who own stock.

That's you.

If Coca-Cola decides to divide the money up, they'll send you a cheque to say, "Hey, thanks for believing in us. And because you own ___ (amount of stock), we want to give you a cheque for $___."

The more stock you own, the more money you get.

This is the "dividend," and it's typically sent every few months.

It's like receiving a paycheque just for believing and investing in a company.

If you're interested, ask your banker about "dividend yielding investments." They'll know what you're talking about and should be able to provide some advice.

And you wanna know something wild?

Some people don't have jobs, but instead, live off dividend cheques they receive from companies they're invested in!

How awesome would that be?? No job, just sit back and wait for the dividends to roll in.

If you're a diligent investor, it'll happen to you too.

And in theory...(get ready for this!...)

You could invest your money through your TFSA, buy a bunch of mutual funds or stocks that pay dividends, and then all the money you receive every three to four months will be tax-free!*

Now you see why I love dividends? They're frickin' brilliant!

I feel so pumped up just writing about them I'm literally buzzing!

...or it's the sugar rush from the Coca-Cola I just drank...

*Small exception here. If it's an American company, they might keep 15% in tax on dividends paid through a TFSA.

The conversation goes something like this:

> CANADA: We have cool accounts called TFSAs.
>
> USA: (*Not really listening.*) That's cool.
>
> CANADA: And inside our TFSAs we can own dividend-yielding investments and then all the dividends we receive are tax-free.
>
> USA: (*Still not listening*) Sweet.
>
> CANADA: That includes dividends paid from US-based companies.

USA: (*Looking up sharply.*) Whoa, what?! Uh, nope. Not gonna happen. US companies are not gonna give you dividends that are tax-free.

CANADA: Ummm—

USA: (*Folding arms.*) Nope. If you invest in US-based companies that pay dividends, then we'll tax you approx. 15% on those dividends before they end up in your fancy TFSA.

CANADA: (*Stubbornly.*) Fine. Have it your way.

If it's a Canadian company, then a dividend paid through a TFSA will be tax-free. Huzzah!

LEVEL-UP ON DIVIDENDS

You might be thinking:

"Doug, this whole dividend thing sounds great, but what if, instead of being mailed the dividend cheque, I want the company to use the money to buy me more stock? Could I do that?"

Oh, hell yes.

Now you're thinking like a financial expert.

It's called a "DRIP," which stands for "Dividend Re-Investment Plan."

Here's how it works:

The company is about to mail you the cheque, but then they're like:

"Oh, wait, this budding financial wizard is part of the DRIP which means they want us to buy more stock for them...

...Okay, how much is their dividend? Right, that'll buy them 'X' number of shares. Done."

Every time this happens, the number of shares you own goes up.

Which means in three to four months, the next dividend will be worth even more. The one after that, even more.

It's compounding. Just like Golden Rule #3, Snowball Compound Interest.

Frickin' brilliant.

And if you decide to stop the DRIP for a while and have the cheque mailed to you, you can absolutely do that. It's your money.

You want the DRIP to start up again? No problem.

Small tangent:

I actually love the acronym "DRIP" because I have this image of an icicle dripping.

If the drop of water falls off the icicle, it's lost, it's gone. That would be like receiving your dividend cheque and spending it.

B'bye.

But if the drop of water hangs on long enough, it'll freeze and the icicle gets bigger.

When you use a DRIP in your own investing, your money grows and grows and grows.

Compound interest to the extreme. *Love. It.*

YOUR PARENTS #2

Wow. We've covered a lot.

We're only at the end of Chunk #2 and you already know the pathway to becoming a millionaire and all about the stock market.

(And you know about ski slopes! Whodathunk?)

It would be cool if the conversation with your parents evolves to chatting about investments.

Do they have any investments themselves? If so, what are they invested in?

What level of risk do they feel they're at with their investments? Green Circle? Blue Square? Black Diamond?

(You might have to explain the analogy.)

And the fun question: How do they feel about dividends? Are they receiving any?

If they are, does it feel like an extra payday every three to four months? Do they jump up and down?

Hopefully by now your parents have recognized your burgeoning interest in all this stuff and they're thrilled you're reading this book.

Also, I'm totally bringing back the word "burgeoning." Such a great word.

Speaking of words, the word "retirement" has probably come up in conversations.

As in, your parents might have an account called the "Registered Retirement Savings Plan" or "RRSP."

Doug wipes his brow and breathes deep in preparation

…I guess…we need to talk about this one…

…because you kinda need to know about the RRSP if you're gonna be a millionaire…

Okay, can I be honest? …I'm nervous. Like, really nervous.

Every time I attempt to explain the RRSP, I'm reminded of how unbelievably complicated it is.

Sure, the basic concept is simple: You're saving money for retirement. Great!

But as we dive deeper, you'll see how it can get confusing.

And it's particularly difficult to teach because it's a "chicken-or-the-egg" kind of scenario.

As in, you need to know X before you can understand Y, but you need to know Y before you can understand X.

Challenging, obviously.

Are you cool if we take this one step at a time? It'll probably make it easier for both of us.

So…I think…

It's time for a road trip.

Our destination will be the land of the Registered Retirement Savings Plan. But on our way, we'll make a few pit stops.

Our first stop will be to the land of "working a job" where we'll chat about details of your paycheque.

Our second stop will be to the land of "tax brackets." I know it sounds boring—it is. But it's also super important.

You'll thank me later.

Third pit stop, we'll visit the town of "total income and taxable income" where we'll talk about terms like—you guessed it—"total income," and "taxable income."

And finally, after all that, we'll arrive at our destination: The land of the Registered Retirement Savings Plan.

And hopefully it'll all make sense. Fingers crossed.

So that's the road map. Got all that? Feelin' good? You ready?

You grab the car keys and pick out the playlist. I'll grab the water and the snacks.

Vroom, vroom.

Let's do this.

CHUNK 3
THE ROAD TRIP

PIT STOP #1

YOU'RE HIRED.

You just landed your first job.

You applied. You interviewed. You nailed it (obviously). And you got the gig. Congrats!

Pretty soon them sweet dollars are gonna start rollin' in.

Excellent.

Here are some (perhaps-obvious) details:

- You're now 'employed.'

- You have a boss.

- You work for Company XYZ doing whatever.

- You have certain work hours.

- You're gonna get paid for those hours.

And your paycheque will likely arrive every other week.

Now before you actually start working, your company might ask you if you'd like to get paid by "direct deposit."

Direct deposit means your company can put your paycheque directly into your bank account.

Otherwise, they'd have to print out an actual cheque, and those little pieces of paper can easily get lost.

These days, most people get paid by direct deposit. It's pretty standard.

Your company will get you to fill out a "direct deposit form," asking for some basic info about you, your bank, and which account to put the money into.

(Fill it out correctly! You don't want your money going into someone else's bank account!)

Okay, you filled out the form. Now when you get your first paycheque it will go directly into your account.

Perfect.

So now you go to work, you do your job, and you think "I can't wait for my first paycheque!!"

And each day, as you're leaving work, you mentally tally up the amount of money you made that day. (We all do it.)

Over the next two weeks, you continue to add it up. ("How many hours did I work? Multiplied by my hourly pay...")

So you have in mind a very specific amount of money you're expecting to receive.

On payday, you run to the bank. You look in your account. Did your company pay you? Yes they did!

But wait a sec. Something's wrong.

That number can't be right. It's smaller than you expected. They didn't pay you enough!!!

They were supposed to pay you 'X' number of dollars but the amount in your bank account is only, maybe, 80% of what they owe you!

WHAT THE HECK HAPPENED?!

You're not gonna wanna hear this…

…but they didn't make a mistake...

TAXED AT THE SOURCE

Remember one of the very first things we talked about?

*When you make money,
you don't get to keep all of it.*

You always owe a certain amount to the government.

The company you work for (Company XYZ) understands this and they're actually one step ahead of you.

They know you're gonna have to hand over a certain percentage of your paycheque to the government.

So they do it for you.

Your company hangs on to a portion of your paycheque and sends it to the government on your behalf.

This is called being "taxed at the source."

(Think of the "source" as the company you work for—the source where your money comes from.)

And trust me: Being taxed at the source is a really, really good thing.

> Future Millionaire: "But Doug, how is this good?! I wasn't paid all the money I was owed!"

> Doug: "I know it feels that way. But technically, you were. It's just you gotta pay some of it in tax...

> ...If your company takes it right off your paycheque, it's better in the long run."

Think of what would happen if they didn't do this. In fact, I'll tell you what would happen:

You would get a cheque for the full amount of money. For this example, let's just say you made $100.

So you get paid the full $100.

You'd think, "Sweet! A hundred bucks!" and then you'd forget this itsy bitsy teenie weenie detail:

> *You must pay tax on every dollar you make.*

Instead of thinking, "Hmm, I should probably save approx. $20 of this paycheque—*the portion I have to pay in tax*—because the government will eventually ask me for it," you'd end up doing what most people do:

> You'd go out and blow the entire $100.

Then tax season (April) would roll around, and the government would come knocking at your door:

> "Hey, you owe us $20 from the $100 you made while working for Company XYZ!"

And where's that money? Gone.

Your company is doing you a huge favour by taking your taxes right off your paycheque, so you don't have to think about it.

That's good.

Most Canadians are taxed at the source. Your parents probably are—ask them!

> Future Millionaire: "Okay, so my company hangs on to a portion of my pay. Got it. But how much do they hang on to? And where does that money go?"

Great questions.

Every time you get paid, you'll also receive a piece of paper with important info about your paycheque.

This is called a "pay stub."

Most of the time it comes in an envelope. (And most of the time people never open it.)

But it's important.

Open the envelope. Look at your pay stub.

This is information about YOUR money.

I want you to understand it.

YOUR PAY STUB

So you opened the envelope—nice job.

You're now looking at a piece of paper that kinda looks like this (or at least has similar terms):

Employee Name: Future Millionaire				
Rate	Hours	Current Total	Deductions	Total
$16.00	6.25 (6hrs, 15 min)	$100.00	CPP EI INCOME TAX	$5.95 $1.66 $15.00
YTD Gross $500.00	YTD Deductions $113.05	YTD Net pay $386.95	Total Deductions Total Net	$22.61 $77.39

Study it for a second. (I challenge you: How much of it can you figure out on your own?)

Let's break it down starting from the top left:

"Rate" is how much you got paid per hour. In this case $16.

"Hours" is (obviously) the number of hours you worked this particular pay period. In this case, 6 hours and 15 minutes.

"Current Total" is how much money you actually earned. It's your "Rate" multiplied by your "Hours." Like this:

$$\$16/hr \quad x \quad 6.25 \text{ hours} \quad = \quad \$100 \text{ earned}$$

(Now remember: Although $100 is the amount you earned, it's NOT the amount of money that actually ended up in your bank account. That's an important difference.)

The next term you should see is "Deductions." Pay special attention here. This is the "taxed at the source" money.

The word "deduction" basically means "the portion which was subtracted from."

So in this case, this is the portion of money which was subtracted from your paycheque.

In other words, the money
your company did not give you.

Instead, they took this portion, divided it up, and sent it in three different directions: CPP, EI, and Income Tax.

Deductions	Total
CPP	$5.95
EI	$1.66
INCOME TAX	$15.00

Let's tackle'em one at a time.

CPP stands for Canada Pension Plan. (I find pensions ridiculously boring, so we'll make this quick.)

When a portion of your paycheque goes to the Canada Pension Plan think of it like it's going to older Canadians who are already retired.

You're basically paying to buy drinks for some old grandpa.

But to be fair, that old grandpa probably worked hard his entire life and now he's being rewarded.

After you retire, you'll receive some CPP money as well, assuming you continue to pay into the CPP each paycheque.

The government keeps track of how much money you've paid into it over the course of your career.

But now the real question:

How much of your money goes to the Canada Pension Plan? What percentage of your paycheque?

If you were employed in 2024, then 5.95% of each of your paycheques went to the CPP. (Each year, the rate changes.)

In our example, if you earned $100, then your pay stub would say CPP with $5.95 next to it. (As you can see from the image.)

Also:

There's a cap, a maximum amount that you would pay into the CPP each year. In 2024 the max was $3,867.50.

This means that while you're working, 5.95% of each of your paycheques is going to the CPP until the amount reaches $3,867.50.

If it gets to that point (meaning you'd have to be making well over $65,000) then it caps off at $3,867.50. That's the max anyone had to pay into the CPP in 2024.

Make sense?

So if "CPP" is on your pay stubs then you're paying into the Canada Pension Plan and that's a good thing.

Fun fact: You actually don't have to pay into the CPP until you turn 18. So if you have a job right now and you don't see CPP on your pay stub, that's why.

But now you'll know what it means when you see it.

I should also mention that if you're in Québec, it might say "QPP," for Québec Pension Plan. It functions the same way.

And that's it for pensions!

(Told ya we'd make it quick. Maybe I'll write more in a sequel: *Twenty-Six To Millionaire.* Lol.)

The next deduction you'll see on your pay stub is "EI" which stands for Employment Insurance.

When a portion of your paycheque goes to EI, think of it like a few bucks of your paycheque are being sent away to be added to a giant, massive pile of money.

And everyone who's employed pays a little bit into it.

If suddenly someone can't work for reasons beyond their control—like if they're in a work-related accident—some of the massive pile of money gets dished out to help them.

This includes you.

You pay a little bit into this giant pile of money, and then you're protected if something happens. It's a pretty good deal.

But now the real question:

> *How much of your money goes to Employment Insurance? What percentage of your paycheque?*

If you were employed in 2024, then 1.66% of each of your paycheques went to EI. (Again, it changes each year.)

So in our example, if you earned $100, then your pay stub will say EI with $1.66 next to it.

Also:

Just like with the CPP, there's a cap. In 2024, the maximum anyone had to pay into EI was $1,002.45.

Again, in order to get to this point, you would've had to be making over $65,000. But if you were, then the most you had to pay in EI was $1,049.12.

Clear as mud?

Two more quick points on Employment Insurance:

1) I mentioned it has to be a "work-related" accident. This only includes accidents where someone is doing work they're expected to do. Like a cook who gets burned while cooking.

2) You won't get EI money dished out to you if you quit your job or you're fired. But you might get it if you're forced to stop working (like if there's…oh I dunno…a global pandemic, for instance).

And finally…

…the last deduction you'll see on your pay stub…

…the deduction that is going to be the star-of-the-show for the next three chapters is…

"Income Tax."

Income tax is the money we pay for all the awesome public services we enjoy in Canada.

Like public schools, healthcare, snow removal, garbage & recycling, road maintenance, police, firefighters, community centres, libraries, etc.

We definitely pay for all those things, just not directly. Instead, it comes right off our paycheques.

But now the real question:

How much do we pay for those things?
What percentage of our paycheque goes to "Income Tax"?

The answer, unfortunately, isn't as cut-and-dry as it was with the CPP and EI.

If you flip back to the image you'll see that in this particular example, it says $15.00.

Based on that information it would be easy to conclude that 15% of your pay cheque goes to income tax.

(You earned $100, $15 went to income tax, that's 15%.)

In this particular example, that would be accurate.

However, it's not always the case.

I'm gonna expand on this in a second. (The explanation is gonna lead us beautifully into the next chapter.)

However, before we get there, there's a few other details on the pay stub I gotta quickly tell you about.

Check out the image again. Look at the bottom line, on the left. You should see:

YTD Gross	YTD Deductions	YTD Net pay
$500.00	$113.05	$386.95

YTD stands for "year to date."

(Hey, this is familiar! We talked about YTD in the Mutual Funds chapter.)

"YTD Gross" is the total amount of money you've earned from your company since January 1st.

"YTD Deductions" is the total amount of money your company has withheld (taxed you at source) since January 1st.

(In other words, the total amount of money you've already paid in CPP, EI and Income Tax since the beginning of the year.)

And finally, "YTD Net pay" is the total amount of money that has *actually ended up in your bank account* since January 1st.

Another way to think about these three terms is:

YTD Gross — YTD Deductions = YTD Net pay

And the last detail on the paystub (we're almost done!) is in the bottom right corner:

Total Deductions	$22.61
Total Net	$77.39

Total Deductions is all your deductions from this specific paycheque added up. ($5.95 + $1.66 + $15.00)

Total Net is the amount of money you earned minus all the deductions.

In other words, this is the amount of money that actually ended up in your bank account.

Pretty important number, I'd say.

And that's it for the pay stub! Hope all that is making sense.

You can always refer back to this chapter the next time you get paid. (Make sure you open the envelope!)

So now let's get back to our question regarding income tax:

How much do we pay for all those public services?
What percentage of our paycheque goes to "Income Tax"?

The answer is slightly complicated: It all depends on how much money we earn throughout the year.

The more money we make, the more taxes we pay.

And the government puts us in different categories based on how much we're earning.

These categories are called "tax brackets."

And can I tell you a secret?

Most Canadians, in my experience, *have no idea how they actually work.*

Sure, some people know… but most don't.
(And to be fair, it's not their fault; tax brackets are tricky.)

But here's the good news: I'm gonna show ya.

And get yourself ready.

It's highly likely you're about to become
smarter than most people in Canada.

Let's hop back in the car. Bring on pit stop #2.

Vroom, vroom.

PIT STOP #2

TAX BRACKETS

In Canada, the more money you make, the more taxes you pay.

Basically.

This means rich people (who can afford it) pay the most in taxes, and the rest of us pay less.

But regardless of how much money you make, you have to pay a certain amount in tax.

At the beginning of the book we used the example of 20%. So if you made $100, then $20 went to the government.

That was the simple way of thinking about it.

But now you know that from each paycheque we gotta pay CPP and EI.

So the question remains: How much of our paycheque do we have to pay in income tax?

That's gonna be the main focus of this chapter.

Here's the thing: It all depends on how much we're making.

And we use these things called "tax brackets" to show us how much we actually gotta pay.

Check it out:

TAX BRACKETS IN CANADA 2024 (FEDERAL)	
Amount of Tax paid on last dollar made	Annual Income
15%	$0.00 - $55,867
20.5%	more than $55,867, up to $111,733
26%	more than $111,733, up to $173,205
29%	more than $173,205, up to $246,752
33%	over $246,752

So what does this chart mean?

It means in 2024, if you earned $55,867 or less, then 15% of whatever you made goes to income tax.

Or we'd say you're in the "15% tax bracket."

The math is pretty simple, right? If you make $55,867 or less, you pay 15% in taxes. Easy-peasy.

Now, just for fun, what if I asked you:

"If I make $115,000, which tax bracket do I fall in? And how much do I have to pay in tax?"

You'd look at the chart.

"Alright Doug," you would say, "you fall in the 26% tax bracket, so you gotta pay 26% of $115,000. So $29,900 altogether."

And I would say: "Uh…not quite."

And you'd be like, "What!? But that's what the chart says!"

It's about to get complicated. Put your thinking cap on.

If I make $115,000 in a year, *the first $55,867 I will be taxed at 15%.*

After that, *the money I make between $55,867 - $111,733 I will be taxed at 20.5%.*

After that, *the money I make between $111,733 - $115,000 I will be taxed at 26%.*

I know, I know…

You're thinking, "What the *bleep* is going on?!?!" Told ya it was complicated.

But trust me, this system is way better than having to pay $29,900 in taxes if you make $115,000.

Instead, the government divides your $115,000 into three chunks. (Reminder: These are 2024 numbers. It changes slightly each year.)

CHUNK 1
(TOTAL OF $55,867)

CHUNK 2
(TOTAL OF $55,866)

CHUNK 3
(TOTAL OF $3,267)

Chunk 1 they tax you at 15%.

Chunk 2 they tax you at 20.5%.

Chunk 3 they tax you at 26%.

So let's do the math.

    Chunk 1: $55,867 x 0.15 = $8,380.05

    Chunk 2: $55,866 x 0.205 = $11,452.53

    Chunk 3: $3,267 x 0.26 = $849.42

If you add it all up, the amount of tax the government wants from you is $20,682.

It's still a lot of money, but I mean, c'mon, that's *way* better than $29,900.

Now, you might be asking, "Why do they do this? Why break it up into three chunks? Why not just tax the entire salary at the tax bracket percentage?"

Good questions.

Doing it like this is the government's way of trying to keep things "fair."

Let's look at it from a different angle.

Pretend we live in a fictional world where the tax bracket you fall into indicates the percentage of your salary you have to pay in income tax.

As in, if you're making $115,000, you have to pay $29,900.

Let's compare Hillary and John. (And FYI, I'm gonna round to the nearest dollar.)

In this pretend world, Hillary is making $55,867, so *exactly* inside the first tax bracket. She would be paying 15% in tax, so $8,380.

Then you have John, who is making $55,868, so literally only *one dollar* more than Hillary, but he falls in the 20.5% tax bracket.

In this pretend world, John's entire salary would be taxed at 20.5% ($55,868 x 20.5%), which means he would have to pay $11,453 in taxes.

So Hillary is making $55,867 and paying $8,380 in taxes.

John is making only *one dollar* more than Hillary but he has to pay $11,453 in taxes. That's over $3,000 more!

Uh…that doesn't seem right. Luckily, that's not how our system works.

Back to the real world. Instead of John's entire salary being taxed at 20.5%, it would be divided into two chunks.

CHUNK 1
$55,867

CHUNK 2
$1.00

Chunk 1 gets taxed at 15%, like this:

$$\$55,867 \ \times \ 15\% = \$8,380$$

Chunk 2 gets taxed at 20.5%, like this:

$$\$1.00 \ \times \ 20.5\% \ = \ \$0.205$$

And then we add them together:

$$\$8,380 \ + \ \$0.205 \ = \ \$8,380.205 \ \text{(rounded up to } \$8,380.21)$$

So John pays $8,380.21 in taxes rather than $11,453.

That's way better. This is why tax brackets matter.

Now, I wanna clarify something:

In our first example, we used the number $115,000 and checked the tax bracket chart to see which bracket we're in.

In our second example with Hillary and John, we used the number $55,867 to check the tax bracket chart to see which bracket we're in.

This number—*the number we use to check the tax bracket chart*—is what we're gonna call our "taxable income."

This is very important to understand.

We do not—I repeat, we DO NOT—check the tax bracket chart until we've calculated our "taxable income."

We go through a couple steps to calculate this number, but once we have it, *that's when we check the chart.*

Sound good?

So for now, I want you to remember the term "taxable income."

Burn it into your memory. I'm gonna test you on it. "Taxable income." More on this when we get to Pit Stop #3.

But before we leave Pit Stop #2, I wanna tell you about a *HUGE* mistake people make. Like, massive.

Especially if they don't understand tax brackets...

P.S. I wanna quickly mention that we're only working with the federal tax bracket chart in these examples.

All the provinces/territories have their own tax bracket chart which is calculated and charged on top of the federal chart.

> Future Millionaire: "So Doug, does that mean people pay different amounts of income tax depending on which province/territory they live in?"
>
> Doug: "Yessiree bob."

But for now, to keep things simple, we're gonna go with the federal numbers. (The numbers that apply to everyone.)

DON'T MAKE THIS MISTAKE!

What was the term I asked you to remember? DON'T LOOK BACK!

Still got it? Good. Told ya I'd test ya on it. :)

So, I know this guy…I won't say who…***coughs***…just some guy I know really well…

He once had a job that paid him an annual salary that came in *just under* one of the tax bracket cutoffs.

For the sake of this story, I'll use the 2024 tax bracket numbers. So this guy I'm talking about (…who is definitely not me…) was making $55,000.

This means he fell just inside the 15% tax bracket, paying $8,250 a year in tax (15% of $55,000).

Now at the time, this particular guy didn't understand tax brackets. Like, at all. ...fool.

But then something awesome happened: His boss offered him a raise of $2,000!

Which would bring his income up to $57,000. Sweet!

Now, this guy was excited about his raise, except he had started to read about these things called "tax brackets" and like I said, *he didn't understand them at all.*

Here's where the mistake happened.

This guy knew he was paying 15% of $55,000 ($8,250) in taxes every year.

He knew just enough about tax brackets to know that a raise of $2,000 would bump him into a higher tax bracket and— here comes the mistake—*he foolishly assumed his ENTIRE salary would be taxed at the new rate.*

He made the following *INCORRECT* calculation and assumption:

He thought if he was bumped into the next tax bracket (20.5%), he would be paying 20.5% on his *entire* new salary of $57,000.

This would work out to a new tax payment of $11,685.

Remember: Before the raise, he was paying $8,250 in taxes. And now he thought he'd be paying $11,685.

Make sense?

He thought, as a result of the pay raise, he would be paying over $3,000 *more* in taxes, yet his salary was only increasing by $2,000.

Well, this didn't seem like a good thing to him at all.

SO THE FOOL ACTUALLY
TURNED DOWN THE PAY RAISE!!!

slaps forehead, shakes head in horror and disgust

If you're beginning to understand tax brackets you'll see why this is the DUMBEST thing he could have done.

General rule: NEVER TURN DOWN A PAY RAISE.

So where did he mess up and what would have actually happened?

He messed up because he didn't read this book. You're already ahead of him. Well done.

Here's what would have actually happened:

With his new annual salary of $57,000, the government would have divided it into two chunks:

CHUNK 1   # CHUNK 2

$55,867 $1,133

Chunk 1 the government would've taxed at 15%, for a total of $8,380.05.

Chunk 2 the government would've taxed at 20.5%, for a total of $232.27.

Add'em up.

With a new annual salary of $57,000, he would have had to pay $8,612.32 in taxes.

Which means a raise of $2,000 would have resulted in an increase of $362.32 to his taxes.

This guy (the idiot) turned down an extra $1,637.68 in his pocket every year! He was just like *meh* no thanks.

No wonder ~~my~~ *his* boss was so confused.

Bottom line: Don't turn down a pay raise.

If it bumps you into the next tax bracket, that's okay! The system we have in Canada encourages pay raises.

How ridiculous would it be if our system discouraged getting paid more?!

Like I said, there are many people who don't understand how tax brackets work. I don't want you to be one of them.

Okay, good pit stop. I feel refueled (or recharged if we're driving an electric car).

Onwards!

Vroom, vroom. (Or…? Silence, silence, I guess?)

PIT STOP #3

TOTAL INCOME & TAXABLE INCOME

Let's pretend it's midnight on December 31st.

HAPPY NEW YEAR!!!

Another year is over. Now is a perfect time to ask ourselves:

How much money did I make this past year?

Let's assume you only had one job (just to keep things simple).

If we took all your paycheques from the past year and added them up, how much would it be?

Hopefully it's a nice, big number!

And since this number is the "total" amount of money you made, we're gonna call this number—surprise, surprise—your "total Income."

So the term "total income" is easy enough to understand. It's the total amount of money you made in the year. Fine.

But now we have this other term: "taxable income."

"Taxable income" is the amount of money you're actually taxed on.

(Pay close attention here. I'm gonna show you a little trick that could save you money.)

So if "taxable income" is the amount of money you're taxed on, then the lower this number is, the less tax you pay.

This makes sense, right? The less money you're taxed on, the less you pay in taxes.

But I know what you're thinking:

> "Doug, wouldn't my total income and taxable income be the same number?...
>
> ...As in, if I make a bunch of money, aren't I taxed on all of it? So my total income and my taxable income would be the same?"

To start with, yes. But there's a way to make them different.

There's a way for you to lower the amount of money you're actually taxed on.

Here's the trick:

> *Put money into a Registered Retirement Savings Plan.*

(See? It's all leading us to the chapter on the RRSP.)

Let me show you with an example.

Let's say you have a total income of $50,000. That's how much you made throughout the year.

Normally, the government would tax you on all of it.

But if you put, for instance, $3,000 into an RRSP, then the government will only tax you on $47,000.

So the formula is:

$50,000 (total income) — $3,000 (RRSP
contribution) = $47,000 (taxable income)

Check out this sweet graph:

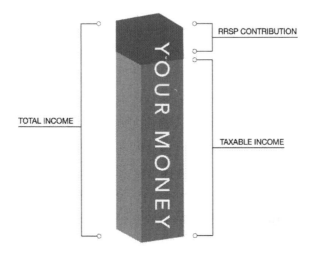

So now you have a taxable income of $47,000.

It's at THIS POINT that you look at the tax bracket chart to
see where you fall. ($47,000 falls in the 15% tax bracket.)

So instead of paying tax on $50,000, you only have to pay
tax on $47,000. Smaller number, less tax. Done.

I'll say this again because it's super important:

Total income — RRSP contribution = Taxable income

In other words:

All the money you made — The money you put into
an RRSP = The amount you're actually taxed on

(Okay, some tax expert is reading this and thinking "Um, Doug, technically it goes Total income — RRSP = Net. Then Net — Other government deductions = Taxable.")

(Yes, Mr./Ms./Mx. Tax Expert, I know. But let's not bore my reader with nitty-gritty details. They just need the basic idea.)

Remember, this is all leading us to the chapter on the RRSP.

So here's what matters:

When you put money into an RRSP, it lowers your taxable income. Which then lowers the amount of tax you pay.

> Future Millionaire: "Okay Doug, I think I get it. But hang on. The $3,000 that I put into my RRSP... are you saying I never have to pay tax on that, ever?"

> Doug: "Eventually you will. But don't worry about that for now. We'll talk about that when we get to the RRSP."

For now, to get us to the next chapter, here's what you need to know in three steps:

1) You make a bunch of money in a year (total income).

2) You put some of that money into an RRSP (your RRSP contribution).

3) The money you're left with is what you're taxed on in that particular year (taxable income).

If you're feeling good with that, then let's hop back in the car.

We've made our three pit stops. We will soon be arriving at our destination: The land of the RRSP.

   ...The chapter that has been making me nervous...

But alas, I can avoid it no longer. Very well.

Big breath. Let's do this.

REGISTERED RETIREMENT SAVINGS PLAN

Let's begin by breaking down the name.

Registered. Retirement. Savings. Plan.

So first off, it's one of those fancy "registered" accounts, like the TFSA.

(Quick refresher: The whole "registered" thing just means the government keeps track of how much money you put into the account, and if you put in too much, they get angry.)

Second, it's an account designed for "retirement savings."

As in, it's not meant for the short term. It's meant for the long haul.

You put money into an RRSP, it grows for like, thirty years, then you take it out.

And lastly, it's a "plan," so...yeah. I guess, like, make a plan and stick to it.

Also, remember how I hate the word "saving" and prefer the word "investing"? It's the same thing here.

The RRSP is really an *investing* account, like the TFSA.

And while we're on the topic of words I don't like, I'm gonna add "retirement" to the list.

Don't get me wrong; I love the idea of "retirement," I just don't like the word.

It's boring and reminds me of cranky old people.

So let's find an image that's a bit more kick-ass. Something to get us excited about using an RRSP to invest money.

How about a bungalow. On a beach. In Hawaii.

Picture it:

Soft warm sand, cool sea breeze, sparkling emerald water, and there you are, lying in a hammock, sipping piña coladas (non-alcoholic, obviously).

Umm... yup. Sign me up, I'm inspired. Okay, let's do this.

I'm officially gonna suggest the name "Registered Retirement Savings Plan" be imagined as:

"Registered Hawaiian-Beach-Bungalow Investment Plan"

YES. Now we're talkin'! Much better. Way more exciting. That's the kind of plan I can get on board with.

So let's assume for a second that you wanna save for retirement—for your Hawaiian Beach Bungalow.

If you use an RRSP it can save you thousands of dollars in taxes and give you thousands of more dollars for Hawaii.

Here's how it works:

Throughout your entire career you put money into an RRSP.

Once money is inside your RRSP, it has to go an extra step and actually be invested in something.

You remember the Walmart analogy with the TFSA?

(Step #1 was walking into the store. Step #2 was actually buying something.)

It's the same with the RRSP: Step #1 is putting money into the account. Step #2 is *actually buying something with it.*

And you can buy anything—bonds, funds, stocks. All the stuff we've talked about.

Ideally, the money invested inside your RRSP is gonna grow and grow. Compound interest.

Money making money. Love it.

When it's Hawaiian-Beach-Bungalow time and you retire, ideally, you'll have a ton of money inside the account.

At that point, you'll start taking money out of the account bit by bit. And that's how you'll pay for the piña coladas.

So far so good?

> Future Millionaire: "Uh, yeah. Doug, this makes perfect sense and sounds pretty simple. Why were you so nervous about it? It seems kinda like the TFSA."

> Doug: "True. But it's about to get complicated."

Remember the whole RRSP contribution thing from the last chapter and how it brings down your taxable income?

Quick refresher:

1) You make a bunch of money (your total income).

2) You put some of that money into an RRSP (your "RRSP contribution").

3) The money you're left with is what you're taxed on (your taxable income).

The example we used was:

$50,000 (Total income) — $3,000 (RRSP contribution) = $47,000 (Taxable income)

I want you to notice something:

In our example, the $3,000 is *not part of the taxable income.*

Which means when you went and put that $3,000 into your RRSP, *you were not taxed on it.*

This is an extremely important point, so I'm gonna say it again. Pay close attention.

You earn a bunch of money from your job or wherever, and normally you have to pay tax on ALL that money.

(Meaning the government is expecting a big chunk of it.)

But because you put $3,000 of that money into an RRSP, you don't have to pay tax on that $3,000.

It's as though the government just pretends you never earned that $3,000, so you don't have to give them a chunk.

At least, not yet.

Now, you remember the TFSA and how when you take money out it's all tax-free? (That's the beauty of the Tax-Free Savings Account.)

It's NOT the same with the RRSP.

This is a key difference.

When you retire and take that $3,000 *out* of your RRSP, *that's when the government will be asking for a chunk of it.*

So instead of being taxed when you put the money *INTO* your RRSP, you get taxed when you take the money *OUT* of your RRSP.

Which is, ideally, when you Hawaiian-Beach-Bungalow (retire).

In my experience, this is one of the trickiest concepts for students—and *everyone*—to grasp when it comes to understanding the RRSP.

> When money goes *IN* you don't get taxed.

> When money comes *OUT* you get taxed.

This is what we call "tax-deferred."

You're *deferring* the tax to a future date. You're saying:

> "Hey Government, don't tax me on this portion of my money today, when I'm putting it *into* my RRSP...

> ...Instead, tax me when I'm sixty-five, when I'm sipping piña coladas in Hawaii, and when I start taking the money *out* of my RRSP!"

> Future Millionaire: "But Doug...why is this good? Why not just pay the tax now, before you put money in the account (like you do with the TFSA)? So then you don't have to pay the tax later."

Good question.

In my attempt to show you why this whole "tax-deferred" thing is useful, I'm gonna make some broad generalizations about people's careers and income.

Naturally, there will be exceptions, but this is the majority.

Typically, people are in the prime of their careers between the ages of thirty-ish and sixty-ish.

During these years, they typically have more "life expenses"—more bills to pay, maybe a mortgage, kids to raise, etc.

These are all expensive things that require money just to live day-to-day.

But when people are in this stage of their lives (in the prime of their careers), they're usually making pretty good money.

And if they're making pretty good money, they're probably falling into a higher tax bracket.

And if they're falling into a higher tax bracket, they're probably paying a lot of money in taxes.

This is important.

During these prime working years, they dream of their Hawaiian Beach Bungalow and they start saving for retirement by putting money into their RRSP.

All the money they put into to their RRSP *does not get taxed at the time they made the contribution.* Again, important.

So they spend years putting money *into* their RRSP. Then they turn sixty-five, retire, and move to Hawaii.

Now they start taking money *out* of their RRSP to pay for the piña coladas.

Because they're retired, they're no longer receiving a paycheque from their job.

Instead, they're receiving a "paycheque" from their own RRSP.

This is a key point to understand.

> *When they take money out of their RRSP,*
> *it's treated like a paycheque.*

And just like any paycheque, the government is gonna tax them on it.

But here's the thing: When they retire, they get to decide how big their "paycheque" is.

And as a result, they control how much money they're "earning" throughout the year.

Which means they control what their taxable income is.

Which means they control which tax bracket they fall into.

> *Which means they control how much*
> *money they pay in taxes.*

> *They have the power! And piña coladas!*

(*Power and Piña Coladas*…I like it. Might be the title of my next book…)

The point I'm trying to make is this:

When you retire and start taking money *out* of your RRSP, you decide how much you take out each year.

And because you decide how much you take out each year, you decide which tax bracket you fall into, and therefore how much money you pay in tax.

So during your prime working years, if you're making a lot of money, then you're in a high tax bracket, paying high taxes.

But by deferring the tax to your retirement years, you can decide to be in a lower tax bracket and pay lower taxes.

This is why the whole "tax-deferred" thing is extremely useful, because it can save you thousands and thousands of dollars.

Okay, how's your brain? Totally fried? We're gonna look at a quick example with some numbers. It'll help, I promise.

Trevor is in his prime working years making $115,000 a year. (Yup, Trev's makin' bank!)

He needs all that money because he's got large bills, a mortgage, kids to raise, etc.

He falls into the 26% tax bracket.

Now, during this stage of his life, Trevor takes a small portion of each paycheque and puts it into his RRSP.

Smart move.

Remember: Normally, Trevor would have to pay tax on every dollar he earns.

But because he takes a portion of his paycheque and puts it into his RRSP, *he doesn't have to pay tax on that portion.*

At least, not yet.

Fast forward. Trevor retires and moves to Hawaii.

Since he's retired, he no longer has the same "life expenses."

His beach bungalow is smaller, he doesn't have a mortgage, he's not paying for his kids, etc.

Trevor doesn't need $115,000/year anymore. Maybe he decides he only needs $40,000/year.

So now he starts taking money out of his RRSP.

(Remember: All the money inside his RRSP should have been taxed at the 26% tax bracket level.)

But now, since he's only taking out $40,000/year, he falls into the 15% tax bracket.

Which means he only has to pay 15% tax on that money!

Sweet! Way to go Trevster!

Making sense? These steps might help clarify:

1) You put money into your RRSP during your working years and avoid paying high taxes on it.

2) It collects interest and grows in value over time.

3) When you retire and take it out, you pay lower taxes.

As mentioned, because of this system, people save thousands and thousands of dollars.

Do I have an exact number for you in terms of how much they save? No. Could we do the math and figure it out? Yes. Am I gonna bore you with that? No.

Just trust me. This system works.

Put money into your RRSP so you'll have thousands of dollars more for when you Hawaiian-Beach-Bungalow.

Okay, let's Level-Up.

LEVEL-UP ON RRSPS #1

So we like the RRSP.

It's gonna save us money in taxes and help us invest for our Hawaiian Beach Bungalow.

Sweet.

But I know what you're thinking:

> "Doug, why would I bother using an RRSP when I can just use my TFSA?"

Smart observation. Here's why:

You remember with the TFSA how you can only contribute up to $7,000? (Approximately. Can change each year.)

Well, with an RRSP, you can potentially put way, *way* more money into it. Obviously, this would be great!

More money for Hawaii! Woot!

So how much more are you allowed to contribute? How much money can you put into your RRSP each year?

This is gonna sound bizarre, but it's actually different for everyone.

Everyone has their own personal RRSP contribution limit.

Here's how it works:

You're allowed to contribute up to 18% of your total income from the previous year, as long as it's less than the current year's RRSP contribution limit (which was $31,560 for 2024).

Don't worry, I'll explain. And I'll keep the math simple.

Let's say in 2023 your total income was $100,000.

The following year, in 2024, you're allowed to contribute up to 18% of that amount to your RRSP.

18% of $100,000 is $18,000.

So in 2024, you're allowed to put up to $18,000 into your RRSP.

Pretty straightforward, right?

But now let's change it up and say that back in 2023 your total income was actually $200,000.

If that's the case, 18% of $200,000 is $36,000.

So it would make sense that in the following year, in 2024, you'd be allowed to contribute up to $36,000.

But the limit for 2024 is $31,560.

And if you contribute more than that, you'd be over the limit, and that's not allowed.

So in this case, you can only contribute up to $31,560.

Make sense?

So officially, for 2024, your personal RRSP contribution limit is the lesser of:

1) 18% of your total income from 2023, OR
2) $31,560

Whichever number is smaller.

> Future Millionaire: "But Doug, what if I don't have a job yet? Which would mean last year I didn't make any money. Can I still put money into an RRSP?"

Unfortunately, no, you cannot. Listen closely.

You're only allowed to open an RRSP the year *after* you first get a job and file your taxes.

Let's say in 2024 you get your very first job. You start making money. Sweet!

Because you're now making money, you are required to file your taxes by the end of April of the following year (2025).

And once you file your taxes, you'll get a fancy piece of paper mailed to you called a "Notice of Assessment."

Your Notice of Assessment has some key pieces of information on it including—and this is important—your *total income from 2024.*

This is the government's way of saying:

> "Hey, we see that last year you made 'X' number of dollars...
>
> ...so this year, you're allowed to open an RRSP and contribute up to 18% of that number."

Make sense?

And once you have your Notice of Assessment, the steps to opening an RRSP will be similar to any account:

1) Walk into your bank.

2) Tell them you wanna open an RRSP.

3) Schedule a meeting.

4) Go to the meeting.
   (Take your Notice of Assessment with you!)

5) The banker will help you open the account.

I should also mention: You don't need to be eighteen like with the TFSA.

There's no minimum age to have an RRSP. You just need to have worked a job and filed your taxes.

Do you know anyone younger than you who has a job?

*They might already be investing for their
Hawaiian Beach Bungalow.*

So to wrap up, here is the order of events:

First get a job.
Then file your taxes.
Then receive your Notice of Assessment.
Then go to the bank.
Then open your RRSP.

I'm really hoping all this is making sense.

Let's Level-Up again.

LEVEL-UP ON RRSPS #2

"I'll start saving for retirement when I'm making more money," said countless Canadians.

Not a good idea.

It's really, really important to begin putting money into an RRSP as soon as you can.

Sooner = Better

You probably believe me, but I'll still prove it with an example.

Let's say you don't start putting money into an RRSP until you turn thirty years old (not recommended).

But then you put in $10,000 a year for thirty-five years and it grows at an interest rate of 7%.

Thirty-five years later, when you turn age sixty-five and Hawaiian-Beach-Bungalow (retire), you'll have:

$1,382,368.78.

Not bad, not bad.

But what if you had started only *six years earlier*, at age twenty-four?

So now you've been putting in $10,000 a year for forty-one years.

Guess how much you'll be taking to Hawaii with you?

$2,146,095.70.

Six years! Only a six-year difference at $10,000/year (for a total of only $60,000) turns into an extra $763,726.92!!!

Mic drop. Boom.

Now, you might be thinking, "Doug, how many twenty-four-year-olds have $10,000 to save each year?"

Okay, fair. Let's adjust the dials. We'll turn down the "ambition" and turn up the "actually possible."

Let's also wind the clock back and start at age twenty.

Now, I'm still gonna suggest that by age thirty, with hard work and reasonable promotions, you could be investing $10,000 a year.

But at age twenty, that might not be possible.

So what's possible? $1,000 a year? That's $2.74 a day.

If you're buying coffee, you can manage to invest $2.74 a day—$1,000 a year—for ten years.

So let's see what happens. You start at age twenty and invest $1,000/year for ten years.

Then, just like before, when you get to age thirty you start contributing $10,000/year for thirty-five years.

When it's Hawaiian-Beach-Bungalow time you'll have:

$1,529,876.43

Do you realize what that means!?

It means the $2.74/day you saved in your twenties—$1,000/year for ten years—could turn into *an extra $147,507.65 by the time you retire.*

WHAT?!?!

Do you know how many piña coladas that is?!?! Hold on, I'm calculating it right now. Average piña colada is $8…

Holy $#*%!!! That's 18,438 piña coladas.

Damn.

I hope you like coconut.

LEVEL-UP ON RRSPS #3

Another quick check-in. You good? If you need a break, take it, yeah?

We've covered a ton.

If you started today reading from the beginning of Chunk 3, your brain is probably pretty fried by now.

Good news: After this chapter, there's only two more in this Chunk. And the last one doesn't require much brain power.

If you need a break, take it. Otherwise…

Let's do this.

Here are three more facts you gotta know about the RRSP.

FACT #1:

As we've discussed, there's a limit to how much money you can put into your RRSP. It's the lesser of:

1)   18% of your total income from the previous year OR

2)   The yearly contribution limit

Whichever number is smaller.

But there's one more critical piece of info:

Just like with the TFSA, if you don't contribute up to your RRSP limit in a given year (i.e. max it out), then whatever room you still have left rolls over into the next year.

This means your RRSP contribution limit for this year will actually be:

A. The lesser of:

1) 18% of your total income from last year OR

2) this year's contribution limit

PLUS

B. Any unused contribution room from the year before.

Here's another super-quick example:

Let's say in 2023, Claire has a total income of $100,000.

The following year, in 2024, her RRSP limit is the lesser of:

1) $18,000 (18% of $100,000) OR

2) The limit for 2024 (which was $31,560)

Obviously, because it's gotta be the smaller number, her limit is $18,000. Fine. Easy.

So in 2024, she's allowed to contribute up to $18,000.

But let's say she only contributes $10,000. Well, that means she has $8,000 of unused contribution room.

So in the following year, in 2025, she's gonna have an extra $8,000 of contribution room to add to whatever her new personal limit is.

Just for fun (and for simplicity's sake), let's say in 2024 Claire made another $100,000 of income.

So now in 2025, her new limit is gonna be:

1) $18,000 (18% of her 2024 income) *PLUS*
2) The additional $8,000 of unused contribution room.

For a total contribution limit of $26,000 for 2025.

Hopefully that helps you understand how your contribution room rolls over and increases your limit in the following year.

FACT #2:

When you take money out of your RRSP, you're taxed on it.

I know we've been over this, but here's why I'm repeating it:

People make the mistake of taking money out of their RRSP to buy a car or go on vacation or something like that.

Bad idea.

Short-term purchases, like a car or vacation, is what the TFSA is for.

If you take money out of your RRSP, you're gonna get sucker-punched with a giant tax bill.

Here's the general RRSP Rule: Don't take the money out until you Hawaiian-Beach-Bungalow (retire).

…With two exceptions…

Exception #1: When you buy your first home, you're allowed to take money out of your RRSP to help with the down payment.

This is called the "Home Buyer's Plan."

You're actually borrowing money from your own RRSP, which means eventually you have to pay it back.

If you don't pay it back (to your own RRSP), you'll get taxed on it. No good.

When you're ready to buy a house, talk to your bank about this (or, again, maybe I'll write a sequel: *Twenty-Six To Millionaire...* we'll see.).

Exception #2: If you decide later in your life to go back to university/college, you're allowed to take money out of your RRSP to help pay for tuition.

This is called the "Lifelong Learning Plan."

Again, you're borrowing money from yourself. Meaning you gotta pay it back, or you'll get taxed.

If at some point later in your life, you decide to go back to school, look into this option.

FACT #3:

This is a weird one.

All the money you put into an RRSP during the the first 60 days of each year (basically, January and February) *actually counts towards the previous year's contributions.*

So if it's the middle of February 2025, and you put a $100 into your RRSP, it actually counts as a contribution for 2024.

I know...weird, right?

Here's why it's done this way:

When January 1st rolls around, people like to look back on the year and figure out how much money they made.

Then they ask themselves, "Hm, did I max out my contribution limit to my RRSP? Did I put in as much as I could?"

If the answer is no, then they still have the first 60 days of the new year to try to top it off.

This is super handy because remember:

Every dollar you contribute to an RRSP
lowers your taxable income.

So by using the first 60 days of the new year to make some last-minute RRSP contributions, you have the chance to lower the amount of money you're actually taxed on.

And if you lower the amount of money you're taxed on then, ideally, you'll pay less tax! Excellent!

> Future Millionaire: "Okay, hold on, Doug. In theory, that sounds good. But something's not quite right here. Haven't I been paying taxes all year long?"
>
> Doug: "Ah, interesting point. Go on."
>
> Future Millionaire: "Well, if I've had a job and I've been taxed at the source, then throughout the year doesn't that mean I've been paying taxes from each of my paycheques?"
>
> Doug: "Yes it does. Keep going. I like where this train-of-thought is taking you."
>
> Future Millionaire: "So if I earned $50,000... but I was taxed at the source...then by the end of the year, haven't I already paid 15% tax on that $50,000? So, like, $7,500?"
>
> Doug: "Yup, that's right. So...?"

Future Millionaire: "So then during the first 60 days of the new year, if I put money into my RRSP...let's just say $3,000... then that would bring my taxable income from $50,000 down to $47,000, yes?"

Doug: "Yes, indeed...so...?"

Future Millionaire: "So then shouldn't I only have to pay tax on $47,000? Which would be $7,050 (15% of $47,000)."

Doug: "Yes you should. But...?"

Future Millionaire: "But I've already paid $7,500 in taxes by the end of the year! So doesn't that mean I paid $450 too much?"

Doug: "Boom. Nailed it!"

You are 100% correct.

In this example, you paid too much. The government owes you your money back.

They'll be sending you a cheque.

It's called a "tax refund."

Read on.

LEVEL-UP ON RRSPS #4
(TAX REFUNDS)

You earn $50,000.

Let's assume all that money is from one job. So you're employed and being taxed at the source.

Which means throughout the year you're paying tax on that money.

By the end of the year you've paid 15% tax on that $50,000. So you paid $7,500 in taxes.

That's the amount you owed, and you paid it.

If that's the case, then all is right with the world. You owed the government $7,500. You paid it. Fine. Done.

But then you decide to put $3,000 into your RRSP.

Now, when you do your taxes, the government says:

> "Oh crap. We charged that Future Millionaire tax on $50,000, and they've already paid us $7,500...
>
> ...But they put $3,000 into their RRSP. So that means we should have taxed them on only $47,000, and *not* $50,000...
>
> ...If we had taxed them on $47,000, they would have only had to pay us $7,050 ($450 less) in taxes. But they've already paid us $7,500!...
>
> ...They paid too much! We owe them money!"

So they send you a cheque for $450.

Put simply: You're taxed based on your taxable income. If you put money into an RRSP, you lower your taxable income.

If you already paid taxes based on a higher taxable income, you probably paid too much, and the government has to send it back to you.

We call this a tax refund and let me tell ya something:

It always—and I mean ALWAYS—feels awesome receiving a tax refund because it feels like you're receiving free money!

(YAY! *happy face*)

But it's not free money.

(oh...*sad face*)

It's simply your money being returned to you.

But it will *feel* like you're getting a bonus cheque or something. So you will be tempted to do like many other Canadians... splurge and spend it.

DO NOT DO THIS.

If/When you get a tax refund, I suggest immediately following these two steps:

STEP #1: Put the entire tax refund into your TFSA or RRSP. Invest all of it. Don't buy the new TV. Invest it.

STEP #2: Congratulate yourself. You just made an incredibly smart decision that most people don't make.

So that's a tax refund.

There are other ways you might receive a tax refund apart from putting money into your RRSP, but those ways are really specific to certain people.

As long as you understand the basic concept, that's what matters to me.

The basic concept:

> *A tax refund is simply overpaid*
> *taxes being returned to you.*

So there we have it! This ends the RRSP journey.

> Wow. What a road trip.

Good driving. I'm exhausted.

We just spent *five chapters* on the RRSP. And for good reason: It's an essential tool in your tool kit.

The jackhammer of hammers!

Understanding the RRSP will help you:

1) Lower your taxes.
2) Invest for your Hawaiian-Beach-Bungalow.
3) Increase your tax refund.

Three birds, one stone. Excellent.

Now, before we finish off this chunk of the book, I wanted to share something with you:

I had a lot of test readers ask me about the RRSP vs the TFSA.

They wanted to know which one was better, which one they should be using to invest their money.

I figured there was only one
way to decide a winner…

GAME NIGHT

It's the Stanley Cup Finals. The series is tied.

The teams? The TFSA vs. the RRSP.

Which team should you be putting your money into? Which one should you use to invest?

Let's see who will win. The puck is dropped…Game on.

TFSA	RRSP
Registered account.	Registered account.
Contributions grow tax-sheltered.	Contributions grow tax-sheltered.
Contribution room of approx $7,000/year. (Changes every year.)	Contribution room of 18% of previous year's total income OR yearly limit, whichever is less.
Money going in has already been taxed (assuming taxed at source). Money coming out is tax-free.	Money going in is money you won't be taxed on that year. Money coming out gets taxed.
Invest in anything, stocks, bonds, funds, etc.	Invest in anything, stocks, bonds, funds, etc.
Contributions do not reduce taxable income.	Contributions DEFINITELY reduce taxable income.
In general, meant for short-term saving (under 20 years).	In general, meant for long-term saving (20+ years).

And the winner is…

You.

That's right. You.

If you're investing money using either the TFSA or RRSP, then you, my friend, are the winner.

I know what you're thinking: "But Doug, which one is better? Which one should I be putting my money into?"

Yes. The answer is Yes.

The point is: If you're using either the TFSA or the RRSP to invest, then *that's* what matters.

Now, there are lots of financial experts in Canada who feel strongly that young people should prioritize maxing out their TFSA *before* putting any money into their RRSP.

I understand their viewpoint. After all, "Max out your TFSA" is one of the Three Golden Rules.

But look, at the end of the day, if you're putting money into either of them, you're on the right path.

So do yourself a favour:

The moment you turn eighteen, open a TFSA.

The year after you first file your taxes, open an RRSP.

It's not that difficult. Yet most people get trapped into thinking, "It's too hard, I feel stupid, I'll avoid it."

But not you.

You can do this. I know you can.

And your future self will thank you. Big time.

Alright, my friend, I don't know about you, but my brain feels totally overloaded with RRSP and tax stuff.

I think it's time we switch gears and talk about something completely different.

On the next page we will enter Chunk #4: The World of Credit. It's an exciting, mysterious, and sometimes dangerous place.

(It's also the shortest chunk in the book. Sweet.)

Should be fun. Let's do this.

CHUNK 4
THE WORLD OF CREDIT

THE WORLD OF CREDIT

Welcome…to the World of Credit.

***Enormous wooden doors slowly
open, Jurassic Park style***

The World of Credit can be a very friendly place as well as a very nasty place. The more you understand it, the friendlier it will be.

Let's explore.

To start with, what exactly is "credit"?

Credit is the ability to borrow money right now, in the present, with the promise that you'll pay it back in the future.

A credit card, for instance, allows you to borrow money right now to buy something, and you agree to pay the money back by a future date. (The end of the month, for instance.)

You're borrowing money and then paying it back.

Do you remember the chapter on banks? Feels like ages ago...

We looked at Group A and Group B.

Group A put their money in the bank and Group B borrowed it from the bank and had to pay it back with interest (the little bit extra).

When you borrow money from a bank or credit card company, you are part of Group B.

Now, before you can start borrowing money willy-nilly, the banks/credit card companies need to first make sure they can trust you.

This makes sense, right?

If Joe Schmo asked to borrow $1,000 of your own money, you'd wanna make sure you could trust Joe Schmo to actually pay you back.

If you knew Joe Schmo had borrowed money from other people and successfully paid them back, you'd probably be okay lending him your money.

But if Joe Schmo had borrowed money and *not* paid the other people back... well, then no-go Joe Schmo.

We have a system that tells lenders (banks/credit card companies) just how likely it is you're going to pay the money back.

It's called a "credit score."

A credit score is a three-digit number typically ranging between 300 and 900.

The higher your number is, the more likely banks will let you borrow large piles of money. So higher = better.

Fun fact: Cell phone companies and car dealerships will also use people's credit scores to determine sales and leasing.

Do you wanna own a car one day? A high credit score will definitely help.

It also helps with more expensive things like a mortgage in case you ever wanna buy a house.

I did a quick Google search. Turns out a credit score of:

- 670 - 739 is "good"
- 740 - 799 is "very good"
- 800+ is "excellent"

So having a high credit score is pretty important. But question:

How do you get your credit score as high as possible?

Answer: You need to build it over time. Like a "credit reputation."

Here's what you do:

You start small. You borrow just a little bit at first, and you pay it off *on time.*

Then you borrow again, maybe a bit more, and pay it off *on time.*

Then even more, pay it off *on time.* More, *on time.* Etc.

If it wasn't obvious, the "on time" part is very important.

Borrow. Pay it off *on time*. Borrow. Pay it off *on time*.

If you do this regularly, you will gradually increase your credit score.

The banks will think, "Hey, this Future Millionaire keeps paying us back on time. We like them. We'll let them borrow more."

Now, there are tools available to help you easily borrow money and pay it off, to boost up your credit reputation.

And one of the main tools available to help with this is a credit card.

CREDIT CARDS

Hang on, pause.

Before we start this chapter, I should quickly mention debit cards, just so we know the difference.

Super-fast: A debit card is your bank card.

If you use it to pay for something, the money gets taken directly out of your bank account.

Using your debit card won't have any impact on your credit score.

On the other hand, your credit card will definately have an impact on your credit score.

Okay, unpause. Let's start the chapter.

A credit card lets you borrow money right now, with the promise you'll pay it back in the future.

So if you use it to pay for something, you're actually borrowing money from a credit card company (Visa, Mastercard, etc.).

And because you're borrowing it, you gotta pay it back.

Which is fine, assuming you do. Actually. Pay it back.

If you don't, you can get into serious trouble. This is why credit cards can be extremely dangerous.

We'll talk more about that in a second.

But first, here's a quick list. Seven basic FYIs when it comes to credit cards:

1) You gotta be eighteen years old to have one.

2) You only need one card to start with. You don't need a wallet full of 'em. One is enough.

3) Your first card will likely have a $500 limit, meaning you can spend up to $500 and then it just stops working.

4) If you use the card to buy something, you now "carry a balance." That's a fancy way of saying "you bought something and haven't paid it off yet."

5) A few weeks after you buy something, the credit card company will be asking you for that money. They often require payment by the end of the month.

6) Paying off your credit card can be done through your online bank account. Your bank can show you how. It should be very easy.

7) There's a period of time between A) the day you make the purchase and B) the day you have to pay it off. This is known as the "grace period." You do not get charged interest during this time.

I wanna emphasize this last point.

If you buy something with a credit card, and then pay it off before the due date—likely the end of the month—you won't get charged interest.

So if you buy something for $100 and you pay back the $100 before the end of the grace period, all you pay is $100.

Nothing extra. No interest. Brilliant.

And that's your way of saying, "Hey, banks and credit card companies, check it out! I can borrow money and pay it back on time!"

This will help increase your credit score. Huzzah!

Furthermore, a credit card usually lets you collect points that can be redeemed for kick-ass products or travel or all kinds of things.

So yes, if used correctly, a credit card can be great!

But now the flip side.

What if you buy something with a credit card and you can't pay off the entire balance by the due date?

Well, my friend, that's when you get charged interest. A lot of interest.

Credit cards can have interest rates of 18% to 22%.

This means if you buy something for $100 and don't pay it off and you forget about it, you could end up paying $118 to $122.

Not only does this majorly suck because you're paying a ton of money in interest, but it also means your credit score can be affected.

Double whammy.

You don't want this to happen. Trust me.

If you find yourself in a position where you can't pay off the entire amount of the card by the due date, at the very least you must—I repeat, *you MUST*—pay off the minimum payment.

Okay, let's clarify what that means. This is extremely important.

If you're carrying a balance of $100, the credit card company says this:

> "Hey, it's the end of the month, you owe us $100 dollars, cough up. If you don't, your credit score will fall!"

But what if you don't have the entire $100 at the end of the month? Oh crap.

If that happens, the credit card company gives you a skeptical look and says this:

> "Fine…if you pay us a smaller amount—the minimum payment—then your credit score won't be affected."

In this example, the minimum payment is probably around $6, which you *must pay on time* to maintain your credit score.

I'm gonna say this again because it's really, really important.

> *In order for your credit score to not be affected,*
> *you must pay the minimum payment on time.*

Okay, let's say you make the minimum payment. Your credit score is not affected. Phew!

But you still have a balance on your card. You still owe money!

That's when the credit card company gets a Grinch-like evil grin and says this:

> "We will now charge you lots and lots of interest on the money you still owe us."

And that's exactly what happens.

So your credit score is unaffected, but you still pay more money than if you'd been able to pay off the whole balance.

Meaning, as mentioned, your purchase of $100 could cost you $118 to $122. Ouchy wah wah.

And here's something terrifying:

If you do not make the minimum payment, not only can your credit score be affected, *but your interest rate can go up!*

Imagine if it went up to 23 - 25%???

That would suck. Like, *really, really* suck.

I don't mean to scare you, but I need to emphasize the importance of paying your credit card off at the end of every month.

Or, at the very least, the minimum payment.

Please pay it off. Please don't be an idiot. Please pay it off.

I'm begging you.

I don't care if you have to sell your prized childhood possessions (baseball cards, doll collection, whatever), make the minimum payment. *On time.*

It's such a wacky world we live in. Think about it:

If you wanna build a good credit score, you need to prove you can use a credit card and pay it off on time.

But this means you *actually have to have a credit card.*

And when you *actually have a credit card* you must exercise two things: 1) self-control and 2) proactiveness.

And typically, human beings suck at both:

1) Self-control: You have a piece of plastic that can buy you almost anything. Need I say more?

2) Proactiveness: You gotta pay it off by the end of the month.

People procrastinate and forget, and then they're in trouble.

You see why it can be dangerous? We license people to drive cars, but we don't license people to use credit cards.

That's insane.

But you, my friend, are reading this book. I have faith in you.

You will be among the smart and educated when it comes to your credit card.

And even if you're sitting there thinking, "I dunno man. I'm no good at self-control and I definitely procrastinate," don't worry.

I got good news.

You can set up an "automatic withdrawal," which is a way to automatically pay your credit card off so you never have to think about it.

At the end of every month, the money you owe will automatically be taken from your bank account and sent to the credit card company.

Set it and forget it.

You can do this by calling your bank or credit card company. They'll offer you two options:

1) A full-balance payment or

2) A minimum payment

If you choose full-balance, they'll take enough money from your account to pay off the entire balance.

If you choose minimum payment, they'll only take what you owe as the minimum payment.

Either way, you're building your credit score/reputation. And that's a very, very good thing.

Okay, that was a ton of info. But extremely important.

Let's Level-Up.

LEVEL-UP ON CREDIT CARDS

Let's say you're in a store, and you wanna buy something that costs $100.

In your wallet you have five 20-dollar bills ($100 in cash), and you also have a credit card (or the tap feature on your phone).

Which do you use? The cash or the card/phone?

You might think, "It doesn't matter." Fine. But me? I'm using the credit card/phone. Why?

Because the thought of letting go of all that glorious cash is too difficult. It's painful. My brain literally goes:

sirens

loudspeaker voice

"WARNING! PAIN APPROACHING!"

"YOU ARE ABOUT TO HAND OVER TONS OF CASH!!!"

Do you know that feeling? Lots of people do. It's definitely not very nice.

So that's if we use the cash.

But on the other hand, if we use the credit card (or phone), we bypass that uncomfortable warning feeling.

This means our brain's natural "brace-for-impact" response simply doesn't happen. Instead, we just tap the card.

Pffft, easy.

So you have two options:

1) Pay with cash and have a nasty uncomfortable warning feeling you're probably not gonna like, or

2) Pay with card and feel easy-breezy pain-free.

Hmmm...tough choice...

So we end up using cash less and less and card more and more. And more. And more. No pain, all gain. Sweet.

I know what you're thinking:

"Uh, Doug, this actually sounds *wonderful!* I thought you were gonna continue arguing *against* credit cards."

I am.

When you use a credit card, you're spending someone else's money.

When you spend someone else's money, two things happen:

1) You go into debt. (Which should really be an acronym for "Destructive Endless Barbaric Torment.")

2) You pay for the "privilege" of using the credit card; the convenience of carrying around a card rather than loads of cash.

And boy oh boy, do you pay for it.

As we've talked about, the average interest rate is around 18% to 22%.

> ...maybe those 20-dollar bills are starting
> to look more attractive...

At the time of this writing, VISA (the credit card company) is valued at $458 billion dollars. That's billion with a 'b.'

VISA absolutely, definitely, most certainly became a massive, multi-billion-dollar company because everyone with a VISA credit card exercised self-control and proactiveness and paid off their credit cards at the end of every month...*

(*My editor insisted I tell you point-blank: that was sarcasm.)

It's human nature to procrastinate. Especially when it comes to things we don't wanna do.

And let's be honest, who wants to bother:

A. Logging into their online bank account ("what's my password again?"),

B. Transferring money over to their credit card account ("am I doing this right?"),

C. Making sure it was successfully paid ("it says it's pending...").

Using a credit card might feel exciting but paying it off definitely does not. So people postpone it.

The end of the month arrives and suddenly the interest kicks in.

Multiply that by millions of people and you get a $458-billion-dollar company. (Did I mention that's billion with a 'b'?)

Here's the thing, and sorry to burst your bubble:

The credit card companies are smarter than you.

They're smarter than me too, if it makes you feel any better.

They know exactly what they're doing and they're damn good at it.

They want you to use the card as much as possible so you'll pay interest every time you don't (or can't) pay off the balance.

They set up incentives; ways to get you to use the card more:

"Use the card and you'll get rewards towards purchases!"

"Use the card and you'll get travel points!"

"Use the card and you'll get insurance!"

It all sounds great. And in most cases, it's all true!

And don't get me wrong, rewards can be super handy! I've used credit card points to buy plane tickets. It's great!

But let's call it what it is:

A trap.

They know if you use the card, you'll probably be like every other sucker out there; you'll procrastinate paying it off.

The end of the month will come and...BOOM. Gotcha.

But let me be crystal clear. The credit card companies are not the bad guys. It might seem like they are, but they're not.

The bad guy is natural human flaw.

We're not perfect. And then we have to pay for it.

A credit card company's business model is simply built on anticipating people falling victim to their own natural tendencies.

Honestly, it's kind of a genius business model. And it clearly works.

But that doesn't mean YOU need to be a victim of natural human flaw.

You have the power to choose your destiny. Choose it wisely.

(Lol, I feel like some wise old monk imparting wisdom. "Find inner credit card peace, oh young one.")

But for real.

A credit card is a tool. Just like a hammer. Used properly, it can do a lot of good.

Used improperly, things can go horribly, horribly wrong.

Proceed with caution.

P.S. One of our test readers asked this:

"Doug, what if I just treat my credit card like my debit card? Meaning I only use it when I know I have the money in my bank account?"

I was like, "Omg, *YOU'RE* the wise old monk. YES. Genius. Do that."

Great way to think about it.

LINES OF CREDIT

Let's be crystal clear about something:

Banks want you to borrow money.

They're in the "money-lending business."

They lend you money, and then they expect it to be paid back with interest (the little bit extra).

So if they lend you $10, they're expecting $11 back. More or less. That's how banks make billions.

Okay, let's think about this.

If they want you to borrow money, wouldn't it make sense for them to try to make it as easy as possible for you to do that?

YES.

That is *exactly* what they try to do.

And one of the ways banks try to make borrowing money easy is by offering something called a "line of credit."

Think of a line of credit as a big pile of money at the bank.

The bank says to you, "Hey, need some extra cash? We got this big pile right here if you want some!"

But don't get too excited, because here's the thing:

Before you can start borrowing millions of dollars, the bank has to decide how much they're willing to let you borrow.

Sound familiar?

They have to decide how much they trust you to actually pay the money back, plus the interest.

The bank is taking a risk. And they're gonna base their decision on three things:

1) Your level of income (how much money you make)

2) Your three-digit credit score

3) Your repayment history (have you paid the money back in the past?)

If the bank is happy with those three things, then it's likely you'll get "approved for a line of credit."

This means the bank is now comfortable letting you borrow some of their huge pile of cash.

Once you're approved and good to go, it's so incredibly easy, it's like magic.

A brand-new account becomes available to you, and inside the account is this massive pile of money (the amount they decided they're comfortable with you borrowing).

Then you can freely move money back and forth from this new account to your own chequing account.

It's ridiculously easy. Which, of course, is what they want.

Now, hold on. When things sound too good to be true, they usually are.

If you get approved for a line of credit, the banker is going to tell you two things:

1) How much the bank is okay with you borrowing.

2) The interest rate on the account.

(Remember, the interest is the little bit extra you have to pay back *on top of any money you borrow.*)

Just for fun, let's say you get approved for a line of credit of $10,000.

So the banker says, "Congratulations, you've been approved for a line of credit of $10,000."

And suddenly a brand-new account with $10,000 becomes available to you.

I know, sounds pretty great so far, right?

Wait for it.

The banker will then tell you about the interest rate and they'll say something like, "The interest rate is Prime, plus 3%."

So what does that mean?

"Prime" means the base rate. The minimum.

As of this writing (2024), the Prime rate for Canadian banks is 7.2%.

So no matter which bank you go with, a line of credit will have a minimum interest rate of 7.2%.

Then there's always an additional rate on top of that, usually around 2% to 5%.

So if the banker says the interest rate is "Prime, plus 2%," what they mean is Prime (7.2%) plus 2% for a total of 9.2%.

Make sense?

Now, this is an annual rate. Meaning over the entire year.

So if you borrow $100 on January 1st and don't pay it off for the entire year (not recommended), then on December 31st, you'd have to pay $100 plus $7.95 for a total of $107.95.

Got it?

Now, as mentioned, once approved for a line of credit, the money is extremely easy to access.

To borrow, simply take money out of the account. To pay it back, simply put the money back. Super easy.

And the banks want it to be.

Hell, they just gave you an account with tons of cash in it; money right at your fingertips.

You wanna spend it? The bank will say, "Go nuts!"

But, my friend, please do not forget: this is not your money.

THIS IS NOT YOUR MONEY.

If you borrow it—*any of it*—you will have to pay it back, plus the little bit extra, the interest.

You're borrowing. You're part of Group B. Which means you go into debt—*Destructive Endless Barbaric Torment.*

It's a very slippery slope. Let me shout it from the rooftops:

Lines of credit, just like credit cards,
can be extremely dangerous.

People get into big trouble. The steps are pretty straight forward:

1) People borrow—heck, it's almost too easy not to.

2) They go into insane amounts of debt.

3) They have to pay the money back plus the interest (meaning they're paying back *more* than what they borrowed).

4) The banks profit off the interest.

Wow, I just realized: the banks are gonna hate me for telling you this.

Whatever.

So how can you spin the system to make it work for you?

Here's how:

When you borrow money through a line of credit and you manage to pay it off *on time*, you can actually increase your credit score.

I know what you're thinking and yes, you are correct, it's just like a credit card.

Borrow, pay it off *on time*. Borrow, pay it off *on time*. Credit score improving.

And remember the whole "minimum payment" thing?

That's the same, too!

If it turns out you can't pay off the entire debt (of the line of credit) by the due date, the bank will ask for a minimum payment.

If you miss the minimum payment, that's bad. But if you make the minimum payment, that's good.

Making the minimum payment can help increase your credit score. Again, huzzah!

That's the upside to having a line of credit.

The downside is (again) this is not your money.

And you can get into serious, *serious* trouble if you borrow it and can't pay it back.

You must be extremely careful.

So let me ask you a genuine question: How do you feel about all of this?

It's tricky, right?

If you borrow money and pay it back on time it can help your credit score.

But if you borrow money and do not pay it back on time you can get yourself into serious trouble.

They certainly don't make it easy.

Which begs the question: When should you actually use a line of credit?

You wouldn't use it for a mortgage, and I don't recommend it for a big purchase. So when should you actually use it?

I plugged that exact question into Google and the best thing that came up was, "For emergencies, or instead of a credit card."

I mean, yes, okay, maybe for emergencies. Maybe.

But the whole "instead of credit cards" thing I definitely understand.

Lines of credit always have lower interest rates than credit cards.

So when you're paying for something, on the surface it might appear to make more sense to use a line of credit over a credit card.

But be careful.

The way you get charged interest on a line of credit is very different from how you get charged interest on a credit card.

I'll explain more in the next chapter. You're not gonna wanna miss this. Trust me.

Let's Level-Up.

LEVEL-UP ON LINES OF CREDIT

Let's talk interest.

The way interest is charged on a line of credit is different from a credit card.

It's important to understand the difference.

With a credit card, you have the "grace period," the window of time before you start getting charged interest.

And if you don't pay off the balance within that time (and the grace period ends), *that's* when you start getting charged.

But with a line of credit, you start getting charged interest the day you start borrowing the money. *Immediately.*

There is no window of time. There is no grace period.

If you take money out of your line of credit, you will start getting charged interest. The same day.

This means if you borrow through a line of credit you are definitely, 100% going to pay interest.

It's unavoidable. Sorry boss.

You're paying for the convenience of having money right at your fingertips.

Check out this example. You'll like this:

Let's say on January 1st you buy two jackets; a blue one and a red one.

(Why two, you ask? Because you're flippin' cold. It's January 1st in Canada. Duh.)

Both jackets are $100 each.

> You use your credit card to buy the blue jacket.
> You use your line of credit to buy the red jacket.

Blue jacket (credit card):

At the end of the month, on January 31st, you pay off your credit card on time (assuming your payment due date is the end of the month).

Because you paid it off on time you *were not charged any interest.* So in total you paid $100 for the blue jacket. Nothing more.

(It should be noted: If you didn't pay it off on time, and just forgot about it for an entire year, you might have to pay $118 - $122. But in this example, you paid it off on time. Nice job.)

Red jacket (line of credit):

On January 31st, you also pay off your line of credit.

But remember, with a line of credit you start getting charged interest *the day you borrow the money.*

Meaning the bank has already been charging you interest every day since January 1st, for a total of 31 days.

So assuming an annual interest rate of 9.2% you will end up paying roughly $100.78 for the red jacket.

(The math is at the back of the book if you're interested.)

There is no option to not pay interest here. You will definitely be charged.

I know what you're thinking:

"Doug, that's only, like, 78 cents in interest, who cares?"

Sure. But if you don't pay it off, that little bit will grow and grow and grow. Compound interest working *against* you.

No good.

Plus—and here's the real kicker—it will impact your credit score, which could start to plummet.

sound of an airplane spiralling and crashing

And like I said: *You do not want that credit score to fall.*

Here's something that will blow your mind:

Let's say you have both a line of credit and a credit card with the same bank.

And let's say you've been successfully paying off your line of credit, but you have NOT been paying off your credit card.

…You ready for this nasty truth?…

Because you haven't been paying off your credit card, the bank is actually allowed to increase the interest rate on your line of credit!

Even though you've been paying off your line of credit!!!

I know, it's brutal! The truth hurts.

But the banks are allowed to do this. It's all in the Terms & Conditions nobody reads.

So if you take out money on a line of credit, try to pay it off as fast as possible.

And do not forget about it! Ignorance is NOT bliss.

Tons of foolish people borrow money and then stupidly forget they borrowed it. But guess what?

The bank does not forget. The bank will never forget.

The bank keeps track of all that interest racking up.

And before these poor, forgetful people know what's happening, they're in debt for the rest of their lives.

Until they die. Alone, cold, broke, and miserable. Fun times.

Last point about lines of credit and then I'll shut up:

(I'm cringing, but I gotta do this.)

There is *one specific scenario* — and ONLY ONE — in which I'd recommend someone take out a line of credit.

Can you guess?

If you're thinking, "Is it when I wanna buy—" No. I'll stop you right there.

For the record: I will *never* recommend taking out a line of credit to make a big purchase.

If you want something big, save up for it and then buy it. (Unless it's a house, different story.)

The ONLY time I'd recommend a line of credit is...(don't make me regret this)...

...When you're already in trouble with your credit cards.

Do not interpret this as me saying, "It's okay to get in trouble with your credit cards."

No, no, no, no, no. *NO!*

This is ONLY if you've already been an idiot and made very poor credit card choices. My advice?

Don't get to this point.

If you have thousands of dollars of credit card debt—
involuntary shudder—you're probably being charged interest up the wazoo.

Horrendous.

If you find yourself in this nightmare, the first thing you need to do is look yourself in the mirror and repeat after me:

"I am a credit card idiot." ("I am a credit card idiot.")

Very good.

The second thing you need to do is grab the scissors and snip, snip, snip those credit cards.

Not even joking. Cut 'em up.

Now, in this horrific scenario, the credit card has been charging you an interest rate of 18% to 22%. But a line of credit would offer you a much, *much* lower interest rate.

So what you'd do is take money out of your line of credit and use it to pay off your credit card.

If you did this, you'd then be in debt to your line of credit rather than your credit card.

And your line of credit will have a much lower interest rate. In our previous example, we said Prime plus 2% (9.2%).

It still sucks, but it's better than 18% from the credit card.

Here's what you do:

1) Walk into your bank.

2) ~~Publicly declare your idiocy to the entire room.~~ Ask for a meeting with a financial advisor.

3) Explain your situation to the advisor. Tell them the truth. Don't shy away from the facts.

4) Explain you want to "open a line of credit to transfer the debt from the high interest rate to a lower interest rate." They'll understand.

5) Hopefully you'll be approved for a line of credit. If you are, immediately use that money to pay off your credit cards.

Maybe the banker can help you right there in your meeting. Even better!

Now, don't misunderstand me; you're still in trouble. You're in debt. But you've transferred the debt from a high interest rate to a lower interest rate.

Still not great. But better.

Moving forward, a small portion of every dollar you earn has to go to paying off the debt.

No, you can't go to the movies.

No, you can't buy the new shirt.

You're in debt *because* you hit up the movies and bought the shirt when you couldn't afford them in the first place.

And now you're paying for it. Literally. Sorry.

If you got yourself into this hell hole, you gotta get yourself out.

Suck it up, princess. You're an adult now.

(Wow, talk about a depressing way to end a chapter. I actually thought about trying to lighten it up but then I thought no, we're talking about debt here. It's depressing.)

YOUR PARENTS #3

"My teenager is a financial genius."

Are they saying this yet? Because they should be.

By now you've basically mastered tax brackets, taxed at the source, total income, taxable income, RRSPs, tax refunds, credit scores, credit cards, and lines of credit.

Not to mention everything else before that!

Holy crap, I just realized...*you're crushing this!*

YOU KNOW SO MUCH! HELL YES!!!

(Hey, you're gonna call me when you're a millionaire, right? And we're goin' for a spin in your Tesla Roadster? Cool.)

Okay, so can we shift the conversation with your parents to talking about credit cards?

Do they know their card's interest rate? 18%? 19%? More?

Do they have a line of credit? If so, do they know the interest rate on it? "Prime plus 2%"? Or "Prime plus 3%"?

Do they feel they're pretty good at paying off their cards each month? Or at least, paying the minimum?

Be gentle.

Remember: Everyone has room for improvement.

Everyone could work harder and be better at this stuff. Including me. (Yes, I know it's hard to believe, but it's true.)

Nobody likes to be shown their weaknesses.

And for many people, their level of financial knowledge is a major (and extremely sensitive) weakness.

Slow and steady. Slow and steady.

Also, I wanna share something with you: Originally, this book did not include these "parent chapters."

Here's why I added them:

Over the years, my students would regularly tell me they had discussed these topics with their parents.

Hesitantly, I would ask, "Really?...How did that go?"

And 99% of them would say it was a bit awkward at first, but they're really glad they did it.

Because those conversations led to smart decisions.

And those smart decisions led to my students finding themselves on the path to becoming rich.

So I decided to encourage it.

I figure if a slightly awkward conversation ultimately helps students achieve their financial goals, it's worth it.

Alright, enough parent chat. Let's switch gears again.

It's the final stretch. Time for some tax slips and life tips.

You got this.

CHUNK 5
TAX SLIPS & LIFE TIPS

IN A NUTSHELL:

TAX SLIPS

You're starting the final chunk and guess what?

You've got mail.

You rip open the envelopes (or open the email) and what do you find?

Tax slips.

You're definitely gonna receive them—everyone does—so I want you to know how they work.

But the term "tax slip" is so boring, I'm dying. It's like they *want* to torture us with these terms.

Tax slips should really be called:

"Special-Pieces-of-Paper-Telling-You-How-Much-Money-You-Made-and-How-Much-You-Already-Paid-in-Tax."

Or the acronym SPPTYHMMYMHMYAPT...

Scrap that, terrible acronym.

Okay, what are tax slips?

A tax slip is basically—you guessed it—a special piece of paper telling you how much money you made and how much you already paid in tax.

But seriously.

It's a slip of paper that gets mailed/emailed to you from your employer/place of work or your university/college.

There are a bunch different kinds of tax slips, but we're only gonna look at two of them:

1) The T4 slip
2) The T2202 slip

Could we look at others? Sure. But they're boring.

And once you've got the basic idea of how they work, you'll be able to figure out the others if/when they apply to you.

Also, before we jump in, I wanna do a quick shoutout to Québec.

> Hey Québec! I see you over there. :)

If you live in Québec, I got some not-so-great news: You have extra homework.

If you live in Québec, you'll receive two sets of tax slips; the slips we all receive and then slips specific to Québec.

That's because you need to file your taxes twice:

1) Federal Taxes (just like the rest of Canada)
2) Provincial Taxes (specific to Québec)

Double the work. Yup, I know, it sucks.

For the rest of Canada, don't misunderstand me; you are also required to pay both federal and provincial/territorial taxes.

But all of it happens on the same set of tax forms, so it kinda feels like you're only doing it once.

Not the case with Québec.

(Sorry Québec! Don't shoot the messenger!)

More on this in upcoming chapters. I'll point it out when we get there.

And I'll make it super obvious so if you don't live in Québec, you'll know the part you can skip over.

But for right now, we're gonna start with the T4 slip. And it applies to everybody.

Bring it.

THE T4 TAX SLIP

So you work for a company throughout the year.

Then December 31st rolls around and the year comes to an end. (Again…Happy New Year!)

At that point, the company you work for will look back on the year and think:

> "Hm, how much money in total did we pay that Future Millionaire? And also, how much did we already tax them at the source?"

Then they will send you a report with that information.

That's the T4 Slip.

It should arrive in the mail/email before the end of February.

And this is what it will look like:

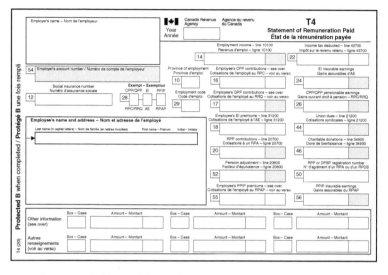

(Image used with permission and can be found through www.canada.ca)

Does it look complicated? Don't worry, I'm gonna show you it's easier than you think.

Check out the top right-hand corner. Underneath the big T4 it says, "Statement of Remuneration Paid." See that?

Remuneration means "all the money." So this means "Statement of all the money paid."

In other words, "A record of all the money paid to you, from the company you worked for, over the course of a year."

Now, notice how the slip is divided into little sections? Little boxes? See those?

We're gonna zero in on a bunch of them.

Specifically:

> Employer's Name
> Year
> Box 12
> Box 14
> Box 16
> Box 17
> Box 18
> Box 22

We'll quickly blast through these one at a time. Buckle up.

Employer's Name: The name of the company you worked for. *(You're like, "Pfft, easy!")*

Year: The year from Jan 1st to Dec 31st in which you worked for the company. *("Pfft, easy!")*

Box 12: Your social insurance number. *("Pfft, easy!")*

Hmmm, hold on. I shouldn't assume.

In brief, a social insurance number is a nine-digit number you need to have in order to work in Canada.

You probably have one. If you're not sure, ask your parents. Keep your SIN confidential. Only share it with employers.

Box 14: Employment Income: In general, this is the total amount of money your employer paid you during the year.

("So all my paycheques, commissions, bonuses, vacation pay, everything added up. Got it.")

Now before we get to boxes 16, 17, 18 and 22, I wanna ask you something:

How well do you remember the chapter on the paystub?

Do you remember how your paystub shows your deductions? (That's the "taxed at the source" money.)

Quick refresher:

Assuming you're employed, your company hangs on to a portion of each paycheque and sends it in three different directions:

> CPP (or QPP)
> EI
> Income Tax

CPP is the Canada Pension Plan.

> You're basically buying piña coladas for that old grandpa who worked hard his whole life.

> When you retire and move to Hawaii, you'll also receive CPP payments, assuming you paid into it during your career.

> (QPP is the same, but for Québec.)

EI is Employment Insurance.

> You're paying a few bucks into a massive pile of money.

> If suddenly you can't work for reasons beyond your control (accident, pandemic, etc.) you can get access to some of the money to help you out.

And lastly, income tax.

> Income tax is the money we pay for all the public services we enjoy in Canada.

Is all this ringing a bell? Hopefully.

Okay, let's think about this:

You make payments throughout the year to CPP, EI, and income tax.

By the end of the year, it would be nice to know how much you paid into each one, right?

It'd be nice to have a record of it.

That's what boxes 16, 17, 18, and 22 are for.

Box 16: Employee's CPP Contributions. The total amount you paid into the CPP throughout the year.

Box 17: Employee's QPP Contributions. Same thing, but specific to Québec.

Box 18: Employee's EI premiums. The total amount you paid into EI throughout the year.

Box 22: Income Tax Deducted. The total amount of income tax you paid throughout the year.

Pay close attention to this last one.

The number in Box 22 is one of the most important numbers on your T4 slip.

Box 22 is the amount of income tax your company has already sent to the government on your behalf.

You've already paid this money in taxes!

So when April rolls around (tax time), the government won't make you pay that money again. You already paid it!

Make sense?

Remember, it's not *you* who fills out the T4 slip, it's the company you work for.

They fill it out and mail/email it to you.

They also mail/email the exact same thing to the government.

Yes, the government receives a copy of your T4 slip just so everyone's on the same page.

So in conclusion:

The T4 slip is very important because it's your company's way of telling the government how much you earned, and how much tax you've already paid.

It's likely you'll receive your T4 sometime before the end of February.

And when you do, I want you to recognize it.

Instead of opening your mail and thinking, "Uh, this looks important…but I have no idea what it is…"

I want you to be like:

> "My T4 slip! Heck yeah! I totally know what this is and how it works! I'm winning at life! BAM!!"
>
> ***Fist pump, superstar pose***

THE T2202 TAX SLIP

"This is arguably the most important chapter in Chunk 5."

One of our test readers said that and I thought, "Well that's awesome, I have to include that, obviously."

Indulge me for a second, will ya?

Are coupons still a thing?

These days, people love gift cards and discount codes, but when I was seventeen, it was all about the coupons.

We'd get these paper flyers in the mail full of coupons for different stores in our area.

The coupons would say things like "$2 off" or "buy one, get one free."

Do they still do that?

Anyway, the idea was you'd grab the scissors, cut out the coupons you wanted, and keep them in your wallet or purse.

Then when you were at the store and the cashier told you how much you owed, you'd whip out the coupons and save mega bucks.

(Okay, maybe not *mega,* but you know what I mean.)

Well guess what? You can get a coupon to use on your taxes.

This means if it turns out you owe money, a "tax coupon" will bring down the amount of money you owe.

Pretty sweet, right?

Question: Are you thinking about going to university or college?

If yes, pay close attention.

If you're a university/college student and you're paying tuition, you can automatically get one of these fancy tax coupons.

This is especially great if you plan on having a job while you're in school.

Think about it:

If you work a job, you'll probably owe taxes. But if you can use one of these fancy tax coupons, you won't have to pay as much.

See why they're awesome?

So every student who is paying more than $100 in tuition can get one.

All you gotta do is prove to the government that you were actually paying tuition. That's it! Voila! You'll get a coupon.

Okay, so how do you prove it?

Your university/college is going to provide you with a piece of paper that will act as your "proof of tuition payment."

And that piece of paper is called the T2202 Tax slip.

This is what it looks like (and sorry the font is tiny!):

(Image used with permission and can be found through www.canada.ca)

Check out boxes 21 to 26.

They show the number of months you were in school (part-time or full-time) and the amount of money you paid.

Again, assuming you're paying more than $100 in tuition, your university/college will send you a T2202.

(Or you might have to download it from an online student portal. Either way, it'll be available to you.)

And this, my friend, is all the proof the government needs.

You show the government your T2202 slip when you do your taxes, and they'll give you a tax coupon.

The coupon will be worth 15% of whatever you paid in tuition.

So if your T2202 slip shows you paid $8,000 in tuition, your coupon will be worth $1,200.

If it shows you paid $10,000, your coupon will be worth $1,500.

Which means when you do your taxes, if it turns out you owe money, the coupon will reduce the amount you owe.

Pretty awesome, right? So why do they do this?

Look, the government understands that as a university/ college student, you're probably so busy ~~partying~~ studying you don't have time to work a job.

Or even if you do have time to work a job, you're probably not making a ton of money throughout the year.

So this is the government's way of saying, "Hey, we know you're working hard and we know school is expensive, so here's a coupon in case it turns out you owe money in taxes."

This is great! The government is giving you coupons!

But here's the thing:

In order to get the coupon, *you must file your taxes each year you're a student.*

I can't over-emphasize the importance of this. You won't get the coupon if you don't file your taxes!

Even if you're making $0 during the years you're a student (which means you will have $0 to pay in taxes), you still gotta file.

> Future Millionaire: "But Doug, if I'm making $0, then I'll owe $0 in tax, so why even do my taxes? What's the point if the coupon can't help me?"
>
> Doug: "Because you will still collect the tax coupon for being a student."
>
> Future Millionaire: "Yeah, but what good is the coupon if I don't owe any money?"
>
> Doug: "You can save it! The government will let you save the coupon for a year when you *do* owe money. We call this a *carry forward*."

As in, you're collecting the coupon and "carrying it forward" to a year when you'll actually need it.

> *But there has to be a record of it.*
> *The only way to create a record is by filing your taxes.*

So let's say you're in your first year of university/college and you don't have a job, meaning you're not making any money, so you won't owe taxes.

(In general, you have to be making money in order to owe taxes.)

But you still want your coupon.

You still want there to be a record of you paying tuition so you can collect the coupon and use it in the future.

So you get your hands on your T2202 and file your taxes. (Remember, the T2202 is your "proof of paying tuition.")

The government looks at your T2202 and says this:

> "Yes indeed, we see you paid tuition, therefore you're entitled to a tax coupon to be used next time you owe taxes."

Sweet.

Then, maybe in your second year of university/college, the same things happens.

You don't owe tax but you still download your T2202, file your taxes, and collect the coupon.

In your third year, same thing. Fourth year, same thing.

Then you graduate.

You're released into the world, and you find a job. Now you're making money.

And because you're making money, you'll probably owe taxes.

But now you got coupons! Four years' worth!

So you do your taxes, and it turns out you owe money. Well now you whip out those coupons and...boom! Mega bucks. (And likely *mega* for real this time.)

Now, I know what you're thinking:

"Doug, this feels like a lot of effort. Finding my T2202, filing my taxes each year when I probably won't owe any money, just to have some coupons later in life. Is it really worth it?"

YES.

We're talking potentially *thousands* of dollars here. Think of it this way:

Let's say you're in school for four years.

If it takes you one hour to find your T2202 each year you're in school (four hours in total), and five hours to file your taxes each year (twenty hours in total), that's a total of twenty-four hours' worth of work.

Let's lowball it and say your tuition tax coupon saves you $2,500. That would work out to $104 per hour of effort.

Like, what?!

Name me a job where you're making $104/hour after only a 4-year undergraduate degree.

(No, seriously, tell me if you know any. I'll be applying.)

I'm trying to drive home a point here.

Each year you're in school paying tuition, go find your T2202, do your taxes, and collect your coupon.

Now, obviously, if you're working a job at the same time that you're in school (or maybe you have a summer job), it might turn out that you actually *do* owe taxes during your school years.

If that's the case, you can use the coupon that year to lower the amount you have to pay!

Basically, if you're in school, you'll get a coupon.

When April rolls around, if you owe taxes, use the coupon. If you don't owe taxes, carry the coupon forward.

Also, if your parents are paying your tuition for you, you have the option of giving the coupon to them.

If it helps them out (by lowering their taxes), this might be worth considering.

The fancy way of saying this is, "You can transfer your tuition tax credit to your parents."

Umm…yeah. Sorry. These "tax coupons" are actually called "tax credits."

Worst. Name. Ever.

But that's what we'll start calling them from now on.

All of this begs the following question:

Are there more ways to receive these tax credit things other than just paying tuition?

Like, what happens when you're no longer a student, you've graduated, and now you're a fully (somewhat) functioning adult?

Are there other tax credits you can get to help lower your taxes?

Yes, my friend, there are.

Are you sensing a chapter on tax credits coming up?

I know I am…

TAX CREDITS

I just feel offended, ya know?

Like, why such unexciting and uninteresting names?

A tax credit is a really, really awesome thing. Give it a name that sounds really, really awesome!

Am I over it? No. Am I gonna suck it up and get on with the chapter? Yes.

So from the last chapter, we know a tax credit is like a tax coupon.

It helps bring down the amount of tax you have to pay.

If someone finds themselves in a situation where they're not making a ton of money (i.e. a student focused on their studies), a tax credit can be extremely helpful.

In fact, *that is the entire purpose of tax credits*: They are designed to help people.

It's the government's way of saying, "Hey, we know you're in a specific situation where money might be tight. Here's a tax coupon to help you out."

Pretty sweet, right?

When April rolls around and Canadians start doing their taxes, the government provides a whole list of situations people might find themselves in.

If you match the description of any one of those situations, you're probably "eligible for a tax credit."

Here's a small sample of situations where people can receive tax credits (there's many more than this):

- You're a volunteer firefighter
- You're sixty-five or older
- You're responsible for taking care of your spouse
- You're a student paying tuition (woot woot!)
- You're a Canadian who is paying taxes

Whoa, whoa, whoa.

Did you catch that last one? "A Canadian who is paying taxes"?

Doesn't that sound like every single Canadian???

You bet it does.

There is one tax credit that every Canadian taxpayer is eligible for. Yourself included.

It's called the "Basic Personal Amount" tax credit.

Now, hang in there because this next part can get complicated and confusing.

I'm going to explain the Basic Personal Amount tax credit in two ways: 1) the simple way and 2) the more complex way.

<u>1) The Simple Way:</u>

The Basic Personal Amount tax credit is a certain amount of money (decided on by the government).

In 2024, it was $15,705.

This is the amount of money you're allowed to earn without having to pay taxes.

As in, if you make less than the Basic Personal Amount, you don't have to pay taxes, but if you make more, then you do.

Make sense?

So in 2024, if you made less than $15,705, you didn't have to pay tax. But if you made more than $15,705, then you did.

It's like the government is saying, "Hey, your first $15,705 is tax-free, but if you make more than that, you owe us."

It should be noted, even if you make less than the Basic Personal Amount, *you still have to file your taxes*.

You have to file your taxes, no matter what. Period.

That's the simple way of thinking about it.

And I hope that didn't require too much brain power because it's about to get much, much more complex.

2) The More Complex Way:

When you file your taxes, you're going to get a tax credit (a coupon) for 15% of whatever the Basic Personal Amount number is.

Let's use the numbers from 2024 again.

In 2024, the Basic Personal Amount was $15,705, so every taxpayer got a coupon for 15% of that number.

$$15\% \ of \ \$15,705 \ = \ \$2,355.75$$

So everyone got a coupon for $2,355.75. Just like that.

You didn't have to prove anything, you didn't have to fill out some special form. Nothing.

All you had to do was file your taxes and voila!

You automatically got $2,355.75 taken off whatever you owed in taxes.

So if you owed less than $2,355.75, the coupon would bring the amount you owed down to $0. Awesome.

And now I ask you:

Do you see why you wouldn't have any tax to pay if you made less than $15,705 in 2024?

If you made less than $15,705, you fall into the 15% tax bracket.

Which means you have to pay 15% tax on every dollar you earn.

So technically, yes, you still "owe tax."

But it's highly likely the amount you owe would be less than $2,355.75.

Which means the coupon you're gonna receive (of $2,355.75) is gonna cover the full amount you owe.

And that would bring the amount you owe down to $0 so you won't actually have to pay anything.

What year is it right now, while you're reading this?

Google "max Basic Personal Amount for ____ (insert year)."

What is the number that pops up?

Whatever that number is, every taxpayer in Canada will receive a tax credit for 15% of that number when they do their taxes in April. Including you.

Long story, short:

If you're making less than the Basic Personal Amount, you will probably owe $0 in taxes.

This is because the tax credit (coupon) will completely cover the taxes you owe.

I'm getting the sense you understand this. But let's look at a quick example, just to be super clear.

And I'm gonna use the word "coupon" instead of "credit" for this example.

Again, let's pretend it's 2024 and you're a university/college student with a summer job, making $10,000.

Let's say this is the only money you make that year.

You fall into the 15% tax bracket, which means you gotta pay 15% in taxes.

$$15\% \text{ of } \$10,000 = \$1,500$$

So you owe the government $1,500.

But you receive the Basic Personal Amount tax coupon. And because it's 2024, the Basic Personal Amount is $15,705.

The coupon you're gonna receive will be 15% of $15,705, which is $2,355.75.

Remember: You owe $1,500. But now you have a coupon for $2,355.75.

The coupon is worth more than what you owe. Sweet!

This brings your "taxes owing" all the way down to zip. So now you owe nothing. Boom!

Okay, I know what you're thinking:

> "Doug, if my coupon is for $2,355.75 but I only owe $1,500, what happens to the rest of the coupon?...
>
> $2,355.75 $-$ $1,500 = $855.75
>
> ...Do I get a refund for $855.75? Should I be expecting a cheque in the mail?"
>
> Unfortunately, no.

The Basic Personal Amount tax credit is what we call a "non-refundable tax credit."

This means you can use the coupon to bring down the amount you owe, but once it gets down to $0, the rest of the coupon is forfeited.

Now, there is such a thing as a "refundable tax credit" which is where the coupon brings the amount you owe down to $0, then whatever money is left on the coupon, the government sends you.

However, the only tax credits likely to apply to you right now are the non-refundable ones.

So for now, only worry about these two tax credits:

1) The Basic Personal Amount Tax Credit
2) The Tuition Tax Credit (T2202)

I wanna emphasize another point:

*We apply our tax credits at the end of
the process of doing our taxes.*

This is very important to understand.

If you break down the process of doing your taxes into six steps, tax credits are at the very end. Check it out:

1) You start with your total income (all the money you made).
2) You subtract your RRSP contributions and deductions.
3) You end up with your taxable income.
4) You check the tax bracket chart to see where you fall.
5) You calculate how much money you owe.
6) Do you have a tax credit (coupon)? Now you apply it.

The tax forms walk you through all this. You won't have to do all the calculations on your own.

So there we have it! That's the chapter on tax credits.

Look, I dunno about you, but it takes me a while to wrap my brain around this stuff.

It's frickin' mind-numbing.

I need to read it again, and again, and again, picking up a little bit more each time. If that sounds like you as well, then hey, all good.

That's the beauty of having a book. You can take your time!

And also, there's no test here; this stuff isn't meant to be crammed and regurgitated on some exam.*

This is knowledge for your life.

You're gonna work hard for your money. I want it to work hard for you.

Okay, you good? Can we move on to something more interesting?

Cool.

*You might actually be reading this as part of your schooling. In which case, there might be a test or exam of some kind.

Study for it.

No, for real. I'm serious. Study your butt off for it. Why?

Because again, this is knowledge you

will need for the rest of your life.

Learn it NOW.

P.S. I'll quickly mention that although the Basic Personal Amount in 2024 is $15,705, it's slightly less if you're earning over $173,205.

Wanted to mention that for the sake of being super accurate.

Although... lol... if you're seventeen and earning over $173,205... yeah... you're probably doin' just fine.

THE RELEVÉ TAX SLIPS

If it wasn't obvious, this chapter is for Québec only.

For everyone else, feel free to jump ahead to the "STUDENT DEBT" chapter. (Or keep reading if you want, I'm not kicking you out or anything.)

Alright Québec-based Future Millionaire, let's talk about Relevés! Woot woot!

Relevés are tax slips specific to Quebec. They function like the federal tax slips (T4 slip) only they look different.

We're only gonna talk about two of them:

1) The Relevé 1 (or "RL-1")
2) The Relevé 8 (or "RL-8")

The Relevé 1 is kinda similar to the T4. This is what it looks like:

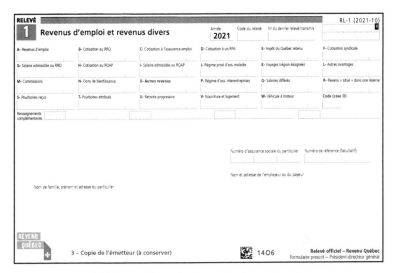

(This image is used with permission and can be
found through www.revenuquebec.ca)

Just like the T4, it's a statement of all the money you made
throughout the year from a particular source.

Most of the time, that particular source is your job.

We're only gonna look at Boxes A, B, C and E.

Box A – Revenus d'emploi: This is all the money you earned
from that job. Including wages, bonuses, vacation pay,
everything. (Yes, you're right, it's kinda like Box 14 of the T4.)

Box B – Cotisation au RRQ: "RRQ" stands for Régis des
rentes du Québec (which is the Québec Pension Plan).

This is the money from your paycheque that you contributed
to the QPP.

Fun fact: The number in Box B should be the same amount
as Box 17 from your T4.

Box C – Cotisation à l'assurance emploi: This is the amount of money you paid into Employment Insurance. (Like Box 18 of the T4.)

Still with me? Wake up! This next one's important!

Box E – Impôt du Québec retenu: This is the total Québec income tax withheld.

> *This is the amount of money your company did NOT include on your paycheque because they knew you'd have to pay it in taxes anyway.*

So they've already sent this money to the government for you. You've already paid this amount in taxes!

This should be familiar because it's like Box 22 of the T4. But here's the difference:

Box 22 on the T4 is the amount of money you've already paid in taxes to the *Federal* government (Ottawa).

Box E on the RL-1 is the amount of money you've already paid in taxes to the *Quebec* government.

In other words:

T4 = Federal, RL-1 = Quebec

This is why, when you're employed in Quebec, you get both a T4 *and* an RL-1. You receive both slips.

And that's it for the RL-1!

Fun, right? (I know… riveting.)

I sense you're yawning, so let's jump to the RL-8 before one of us falls asleep.

The RL-8 looks like this.

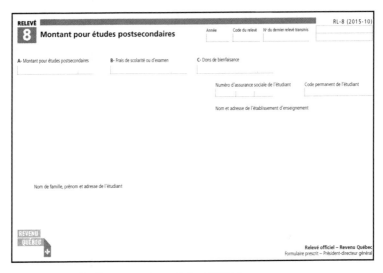

This is the Québec version of the T2202.

Remember the T2202? It's the tax slip you get from your university/college that turns into a tax coupon.

So if you go to University/College in Québec, assuming you're a full-time student and paying more than $100 in tuition, your school will provide you with an RL-8.

There are three boxes on the RL-8; Box A, Box B and Box C. See them?

Usually, I'd explain them in alphabetical order. But... Box A is particularly tricky. So I'm gonna start with Box B and C.

Box B – Frais de scolarité ou d'examen: This is the amount of money paid in tuition and examination fees.

So you (or your parents) wrote a cheque to the school. The amount you paid will appear in Box B.

You can use this number to get a tax coupon to lower the amount of tax you have to pay. (Assuming you owe tax.)

You're allowed to carry this coupon forward or transfer it to your parents if they paid your tuition for you.

Sounding familiar? Yup, just like the T2202.

The coupon you receive will be worth 8% of the number in Box B. (You'll recall with the T2202 it was 15%.)

To transfer it or carry it forward you'll need to fill out a form called Schedule T.

Box C – Dons de bienfaisance: This is the amount you donated to a charity while being a student.

Obviously, there'll only be a number in Box C if you actually donated to a charity while being a student.

Okay, you ready for Box A? This is the tough one.

Box A: Montant pour études postsecondaires.

If there's a number in Box A it will either be $3,537 or $7,074 (for the 2023 tax year).

Pretty easy so far, right? Either $3,537 or $7,074.

Now, before I explain what these numbers mean, keep this in mind:

University is expensive. And there are more costs than just tuition.

There're costs for living, clothing, food, life choices, etc.

Let's assume your parents are helping you out by giving you some money to pay for all those things.

If they are, that's really great of them!

The Quebec government wants to acknowledge the fact that your parents might be giving you some of their hard-earned cash.

So the government is willing to give your parents a tax credit.

It's like they're saying, "Hey parents, thanks for helping your kid out during their education years. Because you did that, we'll give you a little break on your own taxes."

So how much is the tax credit for?

Well, it would make sense if the tax credit was a percentage of the amount of money your parents actually gave you.

BUT WAIT!

Did they actually give you money? Maybe. Maybe not.

Think of the number in Box A as the amount of money the Quebec government *assumes* your parents gave you.

If you did one semester, the government *assumes* your parents helped you out by giving you $3,537.

If you did two semesters, the government *assumes* your parents generously forked over $7,074.

It's just an assumption.

Obviously, everyone's situation is different. Which means the amount of the tax credit is different for everyone.

The important thing is this:

If your parents are helping you out during your university/college years, you can return the favour and help them out by passing this tax credit on to them.

If you pass it on to them, it'll mean they don't have to pay as much in tax.

(You're welcome, Mom & Dad! …slash, thanks for lending me money during school…)

In order to do this, two things have to happen:

1) You (the student) need to fill out a form called Schedule S.

2) Your parent needs to fill out a form called Schedule A.

(I know, I know, "Schedule S"? "Schedule A"? Could they make it any more confusing? Don't get me started…)

These forms will ask for certain information about your specific situation.

And based on that information, the forms will help you calculate what the tax coupon will be.

You (the student) should include Schedule S with your taxes, and your parent should include Schedule A with theirs.

(At least, this is how it is as of 2024.)

And that's it! C'est ça pour Québec.

J'espère que ceci est utile.

STUDENT DEBT

You're seventeen, you probably don't have any student debt.

Yet.

There are loads of other resources and books on this topic. But I'll just cover a few basics:

- Tuition for university/college is expensive.
- You might need to apply for a student loan.
- The funding organizations who lend out money to students offer two things; "grants," and "loans."
- If you get a grant, guess what? You don't have to pay it back! Woohoo!!
- If you get a loan, guess what? You do. Boo. Plus interest. Double boo!
- Make sure you research the different grants your university/college offers because if you can get free money just for being your awesome self, do it!
- Read all details on all forms carefully. Scary fact: Some grants turn into loans if certain conditions aren't met.

- (This means it starts out as free money, but if things change, you have to pay it back. *With interest.*)
- Before taking out a student loan, first figure out *exactly* how much you need (tuition + books + housing + whatever, etc.). What is the total number?
- If the student loan service offers you more than *exactly* what you need...DON'T TAKE IT!!! YOU DON'T NEED IT!!! NO ONE IS FORCING YOU!!! The more money you take, the more money you'll owe. And the longer it'll take to pay off.
- After you graduate from university/college, there is usually a six month interest-free grace period before you have to start paying the loan back.

Okay, what does this mean?

So you graduate. And you have this massive loan to pay off.

I don't wanna scare you but realistically it could be anywhere in the range of $25,000 to $45,000. For many people it's even more! Yikes.

The student loan service says to you, "Hey, we'll give you six months to find a job before we start asking you for all this money back."

They don't always do that, but most of the time they will.

Pay off your loan as fast as you can.

Save every nickel and dime and pay it off! The longer it takes, the more interest you'll pay (that little bit extra).

Here's a scary example:

Let's keep it modest and say you borrowed $8,000/year for four years. So you're graduating with $32,000 of debt.

You gotta pay it all back, plus interest.

Let's say you're given a 3.5% interest rate, and it takes ten years to pay off.

In that case you'll end up paying back $37,972.

So you borrowed $32,000. But you're paying back $37,972.

That's almost $6,000 just in interest! That's crazy!!! (This is how student-loan organizations make their money!)

But what if you could do it in half the time?

If you could pay off the same debt in five years, you'll end up paying back $34,928. Over $3,000 less!

Not to mention the feeling of freedom and relief that comes with being debt-free.

Also, remember credit scores? It's that three-digit number you wanna keep super high so the banks will let you borrow lots of money when you need it.

Well, if you miss payments on your student loan, it can negatively affect your credit score.

No good.

But on the flip side, get this:

If you're successful at making those student loan payments, then not only can your credit score increase (huzzah!) but all that interest you're paying actually turns into a tax credit.

As in, another tax coupon to use on your taxes if you owe money!

The coupon you receive will be equal to 15% of whatever you paid in interest on your student loans.

Here's a super-quick example:

If you paid $100 in student-loan interest, you'll get a coupon for 15% of that amount, so $15.

So next April, if you owe money in taxes, now you owe $15 less. Again, this is all calculated on the tax forms.

This is awesome. And it'll save you money.

I wanna clarify something:

It's not 15% of your student loan *payments*, it's 15% of the *interest* you're paying on those loans.

Big difference.

Each January/February, the student aid service will provide you with an official receipt showing how much *interest* you paid in the previous year.

Your coupon is 15% of *that* number. Make sense?

Also, this is all assuming your loan is through an official government-recognized student aid service.

The student aid programs differ by province/territory.

In Ontario, it's the Ontario Student Aid Program, or OSAP.

In Quebec, it's called Aide Financière Études, or AFE.

In British Columbia, it's called StudentAidBC.

In Alberta it's called the—ya know what? Google it. It's easy to find.

And I wanna move on.

KEEPING A BUDGET

Charles Dickens, the author of *A Christmas Carol* (think "Scrooge"), said this:

> "If you spend more money than you make, your life will suck."

Okay, I'm paraphrasing a bit, but that's the general idea. And he's right on the money.

A smart, strictly obeyed budget can help you stay within your means, so your life doesn't suck. And that's a good thing.

At its core, budgeting is simply about knowing how much money you're making vs. how much money you're spending.

Your income vs. your outcome.

(Outcome? Wrong word. Out goings? You know what I mean.)

Basically, where is your money coming from and where is your money going?

I can tell you this for certain:

The more aware you are of where your money is going, the less it tends to simply disappear without a trace.

The trick is to figure out a system that works for you. And there are loads of different systems.

Different apps, software, techniques, and approaches. Tons of them.

I know, I know, I hear you, but no, unfortunately I can't tell you which system is best.

Everyone has a different way of budgeting, and you gotta experiment to figure out which way works best for you.

It's different for everyone.

But the key is you gotta experiment. You gotta try different methods to find out what helps you get the most out of every dollar.

Recently, I came across two budgeting concepts that I think are pretty cool. I'll share them with you in the hopes they help.

The first one is called the "50 - 30 - 20 rule."

This is a general approach to how you might divide up the money you make. You would assign the dollars to three different categories:

50% would go to "Needs"

30% would go to "Wants"

20% would go to "Debt & Investments."

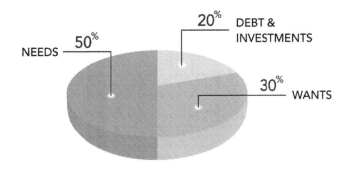

Obviously, "Needs" are the expenses you can't live without. Rent, electricity, water, etc.

They usually don't change much month to month, and they're pretty important if you wanna...y'know...stay alive.

(They're also known as "fixed expenses.")

"Wants" are obviously the purchases you *really* wanna make. New clothes, movies with friends, books by Doug Price, etc.

They'd be awesome to have, but if you didn't, well, you're not gonna die, get fined, or kicked out of your apartment.

(They're also known as "flexible expenses.")

And "Debt & Investments" is money being used to pay off any debts as well as helping you max out your TFSA and RRSP.

Obviously, these are super important. Enough said.

So that's the first budgeting concept I wanted to share.

The second is called the "envelope method."

Here's how it works:

You'd get a stack of envelopes and write on them the things you need to pay for in a given month.

"Rent" on the first envelope.
"Groceries" on the second envelope.
"Student loan" on the third.
"Dog food", on the fourth, etc.

You need an envelope for every single tiny expense.

Then at the beginning of the month, you'd go to the bank, take out cash, and stuff each envelope with the amount of money you're dedicating to each category for that month.

When the time comes to pay for that particular thing, you'd go to the envelope. Once the envelope runs out of money, that would be it until next month.

So that's how you'd implement the envelope method.

Or…at least…that's how you would if we were living in 1943.

Not today.

Today, we have apps and software that help you achieve basically the same thing but they're far more advanced.

One of my closest friends uses an app called "You Need A Budget", or YNAB (pronounced "why-nab") for short.

She swears by it.

She's even part of a group that meets every Wednesday to spend their lunch hour together reviewing their own budgets and staying on track.

They call it "YNAB Wednesdays."

I think this is brilliant. It's an exercise in diligence, and when it comes to budgeting, *diligence is key.*

(I've actually used YNAB myself in the past, and I gotta say, it's pretty great. And no, I'm not being paid to say this.)

These days, for me, I rigorously (and I mean *rigorously*) follow the Three Golden Rules from Chunk 1, and I'm pleased to report I'm doing okay.

But if you can find a budgeting system that works for you and the result is you spend less than you make, then 100% do it.

I don't want your life to suck.

YOUR CRA MY ACCOUNT

Confusing chapter title?

It'll make sense in a second, I promise.

You know how these days you have to constantly create new online accounts?

Like, every time you're online and you wanna buy something or use a new social media website, you gotta create an account.

Then once you have the account, you sign in and it keeps track of all your info and transactions for that particular site.

Sound familiar?

Well, the Canadian government offers this too.

It's called the "CRA My Account." And trust me when I say you're gonna wanna use this service. It's super handy.

CRA stands for Canada Revenue Agency. This is the part of the government that looks after taxes.

The CRA My Account allows you to:

- track the amount of tax you owe,
- track your refund (the money they're sending you)
- track your T-slips,
- see the amount you can put into your TFSA,
- see the amount you can put into your RRSP,
- and do a bunch of other stuff.

This is fantastic! All kinds of info, one easy spot.

But here's the thing:

You know how with the RRSP, you can't open it until after you file your taxes for the first time?

(Quick refresher: First you have to get a job, then file your taxes, then receive your Notice of Assessment, then go to the bank and open your RRSP.)

It's the same with the CRA My Account.

You can't use this service until you've filed your taxes for the first time.

Once you've filed your taxes, you'll receive your Notice of Assessment in the mail.

(It's that piece of paper you receive after you file your taxes that has tons of information on it.)

Once you have your Notice of Assessment, you can go to the CRA website and create your account.

You'll need information from your Notice of Assessment in order to do this.

FYI: The Canadian government website might link your CRA My Account with your online bank account.

In which case, you'd use the same login and password as you do for your online banking.

At least, that's how they do it in 2024. Hopefully it hasn't changed much when you're reading this.

So in conclusion:

I encourage you to use the CRA My Account.

(But your own account, not my account. Your account called "My Account.")

You get what I mean.

Use it.

INSURANCE

Let's be honest, you're seventeen; you probably don't need (or have) insurance at the moment.

So let's fly through this.

Here are two very short chapters on insurance, this being the first.

I'll cover the basics and outline when in your life you should start thinking about it. But then we'll be done, sound good?

Rock on.

What exactly is insurance?

Think of insurance as an enormous pile of money guarded by a company (called an "insurance company").

(Sound familiar? We've chatted about Employment *Insurance* a couple times now.)

When we "buy insurance," we pay for the privilege of accessing some of that enormous pile of money if—and ONLY if—something goes horribly wrong in our lives.

We're buying the feeling of:

> "If such-and-such goes horribly wrong and I can't afford such-and-such, I'll receive some of that enormous pile of money and then I'll be okay."

How would that make you feel? Would that give you a sense of security or relief?

It does for many Canadians. It helps them sleep at night.

We "buy insurance" by making regular payments to the insurance company. We call these regular payments "insurance premiums."

(I know, another dumb name. Why?! *WHY?!* Why not just call them "insurance payments"?! *GAAAH!*)

Anyway, they're called "insurance premiums," and an insurance company usually requires us to pay them once a month, depending on the company and the kind of insurance.

So you might ask an insurance salesman:

"How much are the premiums?"

OR

"How often will I be paying the premiums?"

OR

"Why not just call the premiums 'insurance payments'?"

(Oh man, if you actually ask them that, call me, I wanna know what they say.)

WHO NEEDS INSURANCE?

I'm about to make some broad generalizations and assumptions about you.

Naturally, there will be exceptions.

Here we go.

Right now you're seventeen. The only insurance you might need right now is car insurance. (If you're driving, you *definitely* need it—it's the law.)

But other than that, I have good news: You probably don't need any insurance.

Why not?

Because you don't own a house.
You don't own a car.
You're not working full time.
You don't have kids.
You're in good health.
And no one is relying on you for their livelihood.
(Your dog doesn't count.)

If something horrible happened to you today which resulted in you not being able to work or make money, it would be horrific and devastating.

But no one is relying on you for your paycheques.

Let's pretend you were a parent with a new-born baby to feed. That new-born is *your responsibility.*

> You would have to work.
> To make money.
> To pay for food.
> To feed your kid.
> To keep it alive.

Your new-born is *depending* on you for its survival.

We literally call them our "dependents."

That's anyone—child, parent, guardian, cousin, *anyone*—who relies on you, your job, and the money you make.

They are your dependents. Talk about pressure to bring home the bacon!

Here's the rule:

> *Having dependents = Needing insurance.*

If you have dependents, you need insurance. It's a must.

Because think about it:

If you get hit by a bus and can't work anymore, how is that baby gonna eat?

If you have dependents and you're buying insurance (i.e. paying your premiums), then you're protected.

So when you get hit by that nasty, unexpected bus, the insurance company lets you have access to their enormous pile of money so you can feed your kid.

Phew! ***wipes brow***

And that's it for insurance. Wasn't so bad, was it?

Psssst. Guess what? You only have 3 chapters left in the book.

Crush it.

GIVING MONEY AWAY

Don't worry, don't worry.

I'm not about to guilt-trip you into giving your money to the homeless.

(Although, if you wanna do that, go for it. I have. Feels good.)

Instead, let's talk charities. This won't take long, I promise.

There are THREE AWESOME THINGS that happen when you give money to a registered charity in Canada.

Okay, pause. What's a "registered charity"?

When I say "registered charity," I mean a charity that has done the paperwork to prove it's legit and has received a stamp of approval from the government.

But how do you know if a charity is "registered"?

If you google "CRA registered charities basic search," you will find the charities search engine on the Canada Revenue Agency website.

In the search engine, type the name of the charity you're interested in.

Does it come up? Does it say it's registered?

If so, sweet.

If not, that just means it's not registered *yet*. If it's a new charity, maybe they're still working on it.

The THREE AWESOME THINGS I'm about to tell you only apply to *registered charities*.

(Or…I suppose only the third thing applies to registered charities…I guess the first two apply to any charity…)

I'm stalling, sorry. Here we go.

The THREE AWESOME THINGS that happen when you give to a registered charity in Canada are:

1) The charity gets money to pursue its goal or purpose. Awesome.

2) You get an amazing feeling because you're helping a great cause you believe in. Awesome.

3) The charity will give you a receipt which… (get ready for this)… *becomes a tax credit.*

   Future Millionaire: "Wait, Doug. Does that mean what I think it means?"

   Doug: "Oh, you bet it does."

When you give money to a registered charity in Canada, the charity will give you a receipt.

If you hang on to that receipt, you can claim that money as a tax credit.

This means that every time you give to a charity, it translates into another tax coupon for you when you do your taxes.

It's like the government is saying:

> "Hey, wow, you gave money to a charity. That was really nice of you…
>
> …Tell ya what, we'll let you use the receipt as a tax coupon so you don't have to pay as much in taxes."

Key takeaway:

> *The more you give to a registered charity,*
> *the less tax you pay.*
>
> Awesome.

SO... WHY?

Hey, we're almost at the end! Can you believe it?!

So I've been making a wild assumption:

I've been assuming you started reading this book because somewhere in the depths of your soul you secretly (or not so secretly) have the desire to become a millionaire.

That's awesome! But I wanna ask you something...

Why?

I'm genuinely curious.

What is it about money, or having money, that you find appealing? I encourage you to really think about this.

We all know the saying "money doesn't buy happiness." It's certainly true.

Then why are you interested in it?

(Just for the record, it's okay to be interested. 100%. I know I am. But this is an important question to consider.)

Is it because you like the idea of "being rich"? Or buying nice things?

Or retiring early to your Hawaiian Beach Bungalow?

Or maybe you have an interest in philanthropy (giving money to great causes).

Or maybe you just don't wanna have to eat Kraft dinner.

(Though some might opt to eat *more* Kraft dinner—Dijon ketchup anyone? …If you don't get that reference, ask your parents, it's hilarious, I promise.)

I'll share with you my own fascination with this whole money thing.

It might sound a bit corny, but we're friends now, so I'll just be honest:

For me, money is one of the tools I use to try to create positive and meaningful opportunities and experiences for as many people as possible.

It's simply a tool. Like a hammer.

(I had to bring the hammer metaphor
back at the end, obviously.)

The thought of using money to create amazing opportunities and experiences for people fires my desire to chase it.

It's not the actual hundred-dollar bills.

It's not the sense of pride when looking at bank account numbers—that excitement doesn't last.

It's about all the cool projects and experiences I get to create and offer the world because, let's face it, money helps make projects happen. Nothing wrong with that.

So what is it for you?

You've read my book; you know the pathway. If you want it badly enough, you will totally become a millionaire.

I have zero doubt.

> But ask yourself: *"Why do I want this?"*

If you can find an epic answer to that question, you will live a life full of meaning and purpose.

And then you, my friend, will indeed be rich. In the truest sense of the word.

BOWING OUT

Well, well, well, look at that. You made it to the end.

Hey, listen, I'm really proud of you.

No, seriously. Can we be honest with each other for a second?

This stuff is tricky, and boring, and difficult, and mind-numbing. I get it.

But you did it.

And you, my friend, are one step closer to achieving millionaire status.

Epic.

Also, y'know how when you watch a movie for the second time you suddenly notice all the tiny details?

It'll be the same with this book.

In about a month, I suggest flipping through it again.

Obviously not right now, cause you need a break. But in a month, your brain will be ready to pick up more of the tiny details. I promise.

And the information will be just as valuable when you're eighteen, nineteen…thirty, etc.

I'll leave you with one final thought:

As a teacher, all I can do is open doors. You must decide to walk through them.

If you feel you're one step closer to achieving your financial goals, I'll feel I've done my job.

Remember: There is almost always a direct correlation between 1) how knowledgeable you are about your finances, and 2) how wealthy you become.

In other words, (almost always):

Knowledge = Wealth

The cool thing is you get to decide how knowledgeable you wish to be.

Be smart. Have fun. Get rich.

Thanks for reading.

Sincerely,

Doug

PS. Let's address the elephant in the room. I know you've been thinking it this entire time: My last name is Price and I wrote a book about money.

Coincidence? Yes. Awesome? Oh, hell yes.

THE TO-DO LIST (6 ITEMS)

❏ The moment you turn eighteen:

1) Walk into your bank.

2) Tell the bank teller you'd like to schedule a meeting to open a TFSA.

3) At the meeting, your financial advisor will ask you questions. Answer honestly so they can help you.

4) With their advice, decide on what kinds of investments you're going to have inside your TFSA. Bonds? Funds? Stocks?

5) Ask about automatic deposits so you can automatically contribute to the account.

6) After you leave the bank, treat yourself to something delicious. You deserve it. You just did one of the smartest things you will do in your entire life.

❏ The year after you get a job:

1) File your taxes and collect your Notice of Assessment.

2) Walk into your bank.

3) Tell the bank teller you'd like to schedule a meeting to open an RRSP. Take your Notice of Assessment.

4) At the meeting, your financial advisor will ask you questions. Answer honestly so they can help you.

5) With their advice, decide on what kinds of investments you're going to have inside your RRSP. Bonds? Funds? Stocks?

6) Ask about automatic deposits so you can automatically contribute to the account.

7) After you leave the bank, treat yourself to something delicious. You deserve it. You just did one of the smartest things you will do in your entire life.

❏ Also, the year after you get a job:

1) File your taxes and collect your Notice of Assessment.

2) Go to the CRA website.

3) Use your Notice of Assessment to create your CRA My Account.

❏ Have an honest conversation with your parents/guardians. Be gentle and go slowly. If they wanna give you advice, let them. That's good, it means they care.

❏ If you're in university/college:

In February of each year, get your hands on your T2202 tax slip and use it on your taxes to get your tax coupon.

You'll be able to use the tax coupon to bring down the amount of tax you owe either that year or in a future year.

Alternatively, you can transfer it to your parents to help them bring down the amount of tax they owe. (This is only if you, yourself, can't use it because you owe $0 in taxes.)

Note: If you're gonna transfer it to your parents, you can only transfer up to $5,000/year and it can only be in the year you receive it.

If you end up not transferring it to your parents but instead you carry it forward, then only you can use it in future years, not your parents.

❏ In six months, read this book again.

You'll get even more out of it the second time. I promise.

IMPORTANT DATES WE'RE MIRACULOUSLY EXPECTED TO KNOW

January 1st - The start of the new tax year. It's super convenient in Canada: the tax year lines up with the calendar year. Not the case in other countries.

February 28th (or 29th) - The date that companies are required to have sent out T4 slips. If you were employed in the previous year, you should have received your T4 by the end of February.

The first 60 days: If you put money into an RRSP during the first 60 days of the year (usually up to around March 1st ish), it counts as a contribution for the previous year.

April 30th - Tax deadline for employed people. If you're employed in Canada, you gotta file your taxes either online or with a tax accountant by April 30th.

June 15th - Tax deadline for self-employed people and their spouses. We didn't talk about "self-employment" in this book. But I promise I'll talk about it if I write the sequel Twenty-Six To Millionaire.

July 27th - Doug's birthday. :)

November - Usually the month the government announces the upcoming year's TFSA limit. Usually.

December 31st - The end of the tax year.

RIDICULOUS TERMS PEOPLE USE TO SOUND SMART

"Annuities" – An investment plan sold by insurance companies where you write them a cheque for a huge amount of money. They invest it. And then, in the later years of your life, they give it back to you bit by bit until you die.

If you die before the money runs out, they keep what's left over PLUS all the interest they made from investing it. Follow the advice in this book so you never need an annuity.

"Assets" – Something you own that is expensive and, if you sold it, would probably make you lots of cash, like a house or a car.

"Bearish" – Describing an investor who feels pessimistic about an investment, company or security. They think the price will fall so they're probably not interested in buying it.

"Bullish" – Describing an investor who feels optimistic about an investment, company or security. They think the price will go up so they're probably interested in buying it.

"Capital" – Think of capital as "starting money." So if someone wants to start a business, they need "capital" to begin. The money you use to first buy stocks/bonds would also be considered your "capital." It was the starting money to buy your investments.

"Capital Gain" – If you buy a stock for $80 and sell it for $100, then the $20 you made is called your capital gain. Think of it as the money you make when you sell an asset (like a stock) at a higher price than you bought it for.

"Capital Gains Tax" – A tax which you must pay when you sell a capital asset (such as a stock) at a higher price than you bought it for. A portion of your profit is subject to the capital gains tax in the tax year that you dispose of the asset. However, all capital assets, like all other forms of investment, are tax free inside a TFSA. Sweet!

"Default" – When someone can't (and as a result doesn't) pay off a loan. The payment due date comes, and they can't pay it. Simple as that.

"Joe Schmo defaulted on his loan." This means he didn't have the money. It happens to many people, especially when they're not smart.

I don't even need to tell you what it does to their credit score.

"Diversification" – It's the old metaphor "Don't put all your eggs in one basket. Put them in different baskets." That way, if one basket falls and the egg breaks, the rest are still alright.

In the stock market, this is a way to minimize risk.

It translates into "Don't invest in just one single company. Instead, choose a few different companies so if one of them tanks, the others are okay."

"Equity" – The portion (or %) you own of something expensive.

Let's say you borrowed $5,000 from your parents to buy a car, and you agreed to pay them back a little bit each month until the car was paid off. Every time you pay them a little bit more, you increase your "equity."

So if you've paid them $1,000, then you own 20% equity. When you've paid them $2,500, then you own 50% equity.

You can almost always replace the word "equity" with the words "is the portion that is owned."

"Financial Instrument" – A tool for moving money (in any form) from point A to point B.

A cheque is a financial instrument. Even cash can be considered a financial instrument.

"How did you pay for the pizza?" "The money went from me to the pizza place in the form of cash."

"Financial Securities" – A type of financial instrument. It's a broad term for things like stocks, bonds, or debt that can be traded around.

Don't be confused: There's "financial securities" and then there's "financial security."

"Financial securities" are stocks and bonds.

"Financial security" is when you have enough money to feel safe and you're no longer losing sleep over it.

"Inflation" – If a chocolate bar costs a dollar today, next year the same chocolate bar might cost a dollar and a few pennies. The year after that, it might cost a dollar and five cents.

Inflation is the idea that each year things cost a bit more because money slowly loses its buying power.

"Liabilities" – Debts or IOUs you still have to pay.

Do you owe someone money (including the bank)? If you do, you have a liability. It's a debt you are responsible for paying off.

The root word "liable" literally means "responsible for."

"Net worth" – Your net worth is the amount of money you would have if you sold everything you owned (your "assets"), then took all of that fabulous cash, and paid off all the money you owed (your "liabilities").

How much money would you have left? That's your net worth.

Assets — Liabilities = Net Worth

You can do the calculations to figure it out. Let's say you have the following assets and liabilities:

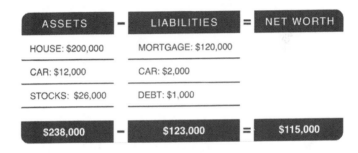

ASSETS	–	LIABILITIES	=	NET WORTH
HOUSE: $200,000		MORTGAGE: $120,000		
CAR: $12,000		CAR: $2,000		
STOCKS: $26,000		DEBT: $1,000		
$238,000	–	$123,000	=	$115,000

So in this scenario, you'd have a net worth of $115,000.

"Publicly traded" - A company is "publicly traded" if you can buy the company's stock on the stock market.

Some companies are privately owned, in which case you won't be able to buy their stock until you're super rich.

"Shares" vs. "Stocks" - Shares and stocks refer to the same thing: A tiny slice of something.

Usually "stock" is used in the more generic sense. We say "stock market," not "share market." Or you could say "I own stock in Tesla."

The term "shares" is more often used when referring to "how many." Like, "I bought stock in Tesla, I now own twenty shares." When you buy stock, you become a "shareholder."

The term "shares" is also used when talking about funds. "I hold twenty shares in a mutual fund."

"Vehicle" - The way in which your money is getting to where you want it to go.

Do you want to invest? You could use a TFSA. The TFSA is the vehicle to get your money into the investing world.

THE MATH

Calculating the interest on the line of credit from page 196.

So we buy a jacket for $100 on January 1st using a line of credit.

We're trying to figure out how much we'll pay in total if we wait 31 days and pay it off on January 31st.

Now, remember, with a line of credit, you start getting charged interest the day you make the purchase, and every day after that until you pay it off.

So in this case, we'll be charged 31 days of interest (January 1st to 31st).

We're using an interest rate of Prime (7.2%) plus 2% for a total of 9.2%.

Here's the tricky part: The interest is calculated on a *yearly basis.*

You don't get charged 9.2% every day.

You get charged 9.2% over the entire year.

So here's what we have to do:

Step #1: Figure out how much we would be charged in interest over the entire year.

We do that by multiplying the purchase ($100) by the interest rate (9.2%). Note: 9.2% as a decimal is 0.092.

$$\$100 \times 0.092 = \$9.20$$

This means if we waited the entire year to pay off the debt, we would have to pay $9.2 in interest.

Step #2: Take that number ($9.20) and divide it by 365 days. This tells us how much interest we have to pay each day.

$$\$9.20 \div 365 = 0.02520548$$

Step #3: Take that number and multiply it by 31.

We multiply it by 31 because that's the number of days we're actually being charged interest in January.

$$0.02520548 \times 31 = 0.78136986$$

Rounded to the nearest penny gets us $0.78.

Therefore, if we buy a jacket for $100 on January 1st, and we wait until January 31st to pay it off, we will be charged the original purchase price of $100 plus $0.78 in interest.

For a total of $100.78.

Hopefully all that makes sense. I admit, I had to get my friend to help me with this one.

I like math, but I kinda suck at it.

SHOUT OUT TO COOL PEOPLE

If you ever write a book, you'll discover, as I have, that it takes many hands to actually make it happen.

I wanna acknowledge a bunch of awesome people:

My family. Mom, Dad, Dana, Greg, Olivia. You constantly support everything, always. It means the world. Thank you.

My incredible test readers. Thank you for your fantastic feedback. This book is what it is because of you.

GROUP #1:
Jake, Juno, Kevin, Mahek,
Max, Nikita, Vitalia

GROUP #2:
Aiden, Alisa, Chiara, Grant,
Haley, Jeremy, Juana, Will

GROUP #3:
Bobbi-Lynn, Camilyn, Draydon, Ioanna,
Isabel, Lora, Lucas, Lucy

GROUP #4:
Brooke, Eliana, Jayden, Lola, Madison,
Megan, Nikita, Skylar, Ty, Vitalia

GROUP #5:
Avery, Chris, Colby, Danya, Ella, Fadilazaki,
Hunter, Jorge, Julianna, Junior, Kathleen, Raghad,
Rami, Riley, Sarah, Sofia, Susan, Tara, Taryn

The National Theatre School of Canada and specifically Alisa Palmer. In 2017, I walked into your office with a stack of books and a crazy idea. You said yes. Thank you.

Carl Pucl, my good friend, and comrade-in-arms. Thank you for all your awesome work formatting the questions and answers for the test groups.

My invaluable content consultants: Hillary Hart, Joel Fishbane, John Willing, Anna Kinson, R. Alex Wyatt, Binayak Pokhrel, Ronika Khanna of Montreal Financial, Stephanie Folahan of Premiere Accounting & Tax Inc., Hasan Salhab of VIP CPA, Taxxlution Accounting (Edmonton), CIBC, H&R Block and the many other financial experts I sought clarity from.

My kick-ass friends who let me talk their ears off about the book for months: Aaron, Monika, Carl, Merritt, Joanna, Sheena, Everett, Rae, Rachel, Alex, Laura, Alicia, Maddie, Mark, and Meghan.

There's more, but you guys got the brunt of it. Thank you.

Christine Lee and Trevor Barrette for starting Writerland, where so much of this book was written. Thank you both.

My editor, Susan Gaigher of Influunt Publishing Services. Thank you for your awesome eyes!

Damonza for the cover design and type-set. You guys demonstrated unwavering patience with me and the millions of tweaks I wanted to make. Seriously, you rock.

My web designer Dave Chisholm (GetCanopy Inc.) and my web developer Colin McDonald. You're both brilliant.

www.seventeentomillionaire.com

My two lawyers, Michael Duboff and Burt Gidaro with Edwards Law. Thank you both for your work securing all the approvals we needed for this.

David Chilton for inspiring this book with your own books, and for the encouragement throughout the process.

The many fantastic baristas and coffee shop owners all across the country who poured the many, many hazelnut lattes.

And finally, you, the reader, the Future Millionaire.

Thank you for gifting me with your time, your trust, and venturing forth on this epic journey with me.

To you, and the wealth that awaits you, I raise a piña colada.

P.S. A little Easter egg if you make it this far in the book:

When your invested money earns you interest, it can sometimes feel like money appearing out of nowhere, unexpectedly, or "out of the blue."

That's what the blue $$$ symbols on the cover represent.

Only people like you, who make it all the way to the end, will know that little tidbit. Don't tell anyone. :)

WHO EXACTLY IS THIS DOUG GUY?

Douglas Price is a master's graduate of the Royal Conservatoire of Scotland and an award-winning teacher and composer (composer? I know…random). He inaugurated the position of the Head of Music at the National Theatre School of Canada, where he (apparently) gave them the impression he knew what he was doing. They even let him start a finance course for the graduating students, making him, possibly, the only person in Canada to teach finance at the post-secondary level without an "official" finance background—don't tell them! After teaching the course for four years and being told it was valuable (anything to shut him up), he decided to write the book he wishes he'd had when he was in high school. If you're reading this, then maybe the book is out there helping people—sweet! When Doug isn't writing, teaching, talking finance or managing his online business (shameless plug: tunetorialz.com), he can be found sipping lattes in one of his many favourite cafés across Canada or hanging out with the people closest to him.

Manufactured by Amazon.ca
Bolton, ON